PRACTICAL
LIGHTING APPLICATIONS
for
BUILDING CONSTRUCTION

PRACTICAL
LIGHTING APPLICATIONS
for
BUILDING CONSTRUCTION

John E. Traister

VNR VAN NOSTRAND REINHOLD COMPANY
NEW YORK   CINCINNATI   TORONTO   LONDON   MELBOURNE

Manufactured in the United States of America

Published by Van Nostrand Reinhold Company
135 West 50th Street, New York, N.Y. 10020

Van Nostrand Reinhold Limited
1410 Birchmount Road
Scarborough, Ontario M1P 2E7, Canada

Van Nostrand Reinhold Australia Pty. Ltd.
17 Queen Street
Mitcham, Victoria 3132, Australia

Van Nostrand Reinhold Company Limited
Molly Millars Lane
Wokingham, Berkshire, England

15 14 13 12 11 10 9 8 7 6 5 4 3 2 1

Library of Congress Cataloging in Publication Data

Traister, John E.
    Practical lighting applications for building
construction.

    Includes index.
    1. Lighting. 2. Interior lighting. 3. Electric
lighting. I. Title.
TH7703.T73   621.32′2   81–13147
ISBN 0–442–24727–3   AACR2

Preface

There are numerous books available on the study of illuminating engineering. Few, however, are written in such a way as to allow an inexperienced person to immediately create their own lighting layouts without first wading through complex theory that typifies most other books on this subject.

The intent of *Practical Lighting Applications for Building Construction* is to dwell only briefly on theories and then jump into practical, on-the-job applications that are used for almost any type of building. It is one of the first books to demonstrate how to use numerous types of lighting fixtures for specific application and, furthermore, how these designs should actually appear on a working drawing.

Architects, engineers, designers, building contractors, electrical contractors, electricians, technicians, and even lighting salesmen will want to keep this book close at hand for frequent reference.

Deep thanks is due to all the lighting manufacturers who provided invaluable reference material and who continually strive for better lighting apparatus to fulfill our current lighting needs.

JOHN E. TRAISTER

Contents

Chapter 1

Introduction To Illumination

Illumination is light on a surface. When this light is distributed with an economic and visual plan, it becomes engineered lighting and therefore practical illumination.

People who design lighting systems should consider them from three basic aspects: quantity, quality, and cost. Therefore, every lighting design or layout should provide the highest visual comfort and performance consistent with the type of area to be illuminated and the budget provided by the owners.

This chapter gives the reader a useful summary of basic lighting principles, along with practical data on how to apply them. An understanding of these principles is considered necessary to give designers a proper background for approaching their work more intelligently. The more important terms are reviewed here for this purpose.

Diffusion: Diffusion is light coming from all directions without preference. In interior lighting, diffusion prevents shadow of any kind and lights all surfaces in the room equally. Absence of shadow in the proper quantity helps destroy texture and form. Diffusion results, particularly at higher levels, in extreme direct glare as shown in Figure 1-1.

Control: Control, as applied to lighting applications, is a planned departure from diffusion; the distribution pattern of the light is intended to accent specific areas, such as those where work is to be done. Control can minimize light that causes direct visual glare and it can create just enough shadow to properly render form and texture. Control may also eliminate reflected glare effects for better work task visibility and more saturated rendition of colors.

Complete control tends to create shadows of too high a density (Figure 1-2), and in general is not conducive to a well balanced,

Fig. 1-1. Diffusion can result in extreme direct glare, particularly at higher illumination levels.

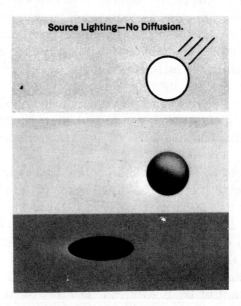

Fig. 1-2. Complete control of light tends to create shadows of too high density.

working atmosphere. What is required is a judicious combination of control and diffusion—control to place light where it is largely needed and to permit adequate perception of form, color and texture, and enough diffusion to soften shadows and "fill in" for what might otherwise result in harsh contrasts (Figure 1-3).

In comparing the illustrations in Figures 1-1, 1-2, and 1-3, it is evident that highlights are missing in Figure 1-1; shadows are inadequate to give enough information about the character of objects. In Figure 1-2, the highlights are excellent, but shadows are too dense to see into. Therefore, some information is concealed. In Figure 1-3, highlights are good, shadows are luminous, and complete information about character and position of the object is given.

Intensity (I): The candela is the unit of intensity (*I*) and may be compared to pressure in a hydraulic system. The term is sometimes called *candlepower* and describes the amount of light in a unit of solid angle, assuming a point source of light. It can be seen in Figure 1-4 that while the light travels away from the source, the solid angle covers a larger and larger area; but the angle itself remains the same,

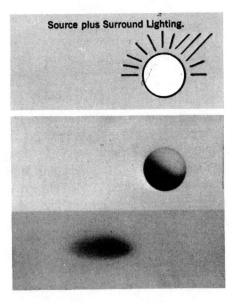

Fig. 1-3. Proper illumination is achieved by utilizing a judicious combination of control and diffusion.

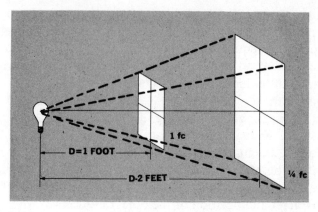

Fig. 1–4. As light travels away from a source, the angle remains the same but covers a larger and larger area.

as does the amount of light it contains. Therefore, in a given direction intensity is constant, regardless of distance.

$$I = \frac{\text{light energy}}{\text{solid angle}}$$

Illumination (E): Illumination (E) is measured in footcandles and is intensity, in cadelas, divided by the square of the distance of the source from the surface

$$E = \frac{I}{D^2}$$

As the area covered by a given solid angle gets larger with distance from the source, the included light flux remains the same. The illumination decreases therefore as the square of the area. This equation is true only if the receiving surface is perpendicular to the source direction. If light is incident at some other angle, the equation becomes

$$E = \frac{I}{D^2} \cos \theta$$

where

E = illumination in footcandles (fc)

I = intensity in candelas (cd)

D = distance in feet

θ = angle of incidence

Light quantity: Light quantity is expressed in lumens and is a measure of the total light emitted by a source or light falling on a surface. It is actually light power and may be expressed in watts. If all the light were green-yellow, at the peak of the spectral luminosity curve

$$1 \text{ watt} = 681 \text{ lumens}$$

This gives some idea of the relative luminous efficacy of common light sources. For instance, a 100–watt incandescent lamp emits about 1600 lumens; only 2.4 watts as light and the balance as heat.

A 40–watt fluorescent lamp emits about 3100 lumens; 4.5 watts as light and the balance as heat. Therefore

$$\text{Incandescent efficacy} = \frac{2.4 \text{ W}}{100 \text{ W}} = 2.4\%$$

$$\text{Fluorescent efficacy} = \frac{4.5 \text{ W}}{40 \text{ W}} = 11\%$$

From the above, we see that the fluorescent lamp gives four to five times as much light as the incandescent on a watt-for-watt basis.

The concept of the "lumen" permits convenient calculation of average illumination from a multiplicity of sources, augmented by reflections from the surrounding walls, floors, and ceiling.

$$E = \frac{\text{lumens generated}}{\text{area lighted}} \times CU$$

where

E = illumination in footcandles

CU = coefficient of utilization

Coefficient of Utilization (CU): CU is a coefficient made up of a number of factors such as room size, shape, reflectances and luminaire distribution. Tables of such coefficients are published by lighting fixture manufacturers and are computed on the basis of using them with the IES Zonal Cavity Method (see Chapter 6). A typical *CU* table is shown in Figure 1–5.

Spacing-to-Mounting-Height Ratio: Calculations using the IES Zonal Cavity Method yield *average* illumination values, but tell nothing about the uniformity of the illumination level on the work plane. Lighting designers, therefore, need to know how far apart various types of lighting fixtures should be spaced, for a given mounting height, so as not to cause any undue variation in illumination level between luminaires. Lighting fixture data should be accompanied by a spacing-to-mounting height ratio figure that gives this information. For example, a ratio of 1.5 means that this particular lighting fixture may be spaced on 15–foot centers for a 10–foot mounting height above the work plane and still maintain a satisfactory uniformity of illumination. Obviously, for a given degree of uniformity, the larger the ratio, the fewer units are required (Figure 1–6).

Luminance (L): Luminance is the name given to what most people may think of as brilliance. It is subjective intensity and ranges from very dim to very bright. Objectively, luminance is intensity in a given

Distribution and efficiency	Spacing ratios and reflectance	Room cavity ratio	Effective ceiling cavity reflectance, R_{CC}								
			80%			50%			10%		
			% Wall reflectance, R_{CW}								
			50%	30%	10%	50%	30%	10%	50%	30%	10%
			Coefficients of utilization for 20% floor cavity reflectance, R_{FC}								
CIE % Luminaire 0 ──┼── 100	Spacing not to exceed 1.4 x mounting height	1	75	73	71	71	69	67	66	64	63
		2	67	63	60	64	61	58	60	57	56
		3	61	56	52	58	54	51	54	51	49
		4	55	49	45	52	48	44	49	47	43
		5	49	43	39	47	42	39	44	41	38
	Maintenance factors Good: .75 Med: .70 Poor: .65	6	44	38	34	42	37	34	40	36	33
		7	40	34	30	38	33	30	36	32	29
		8	36	30	26	34	29	26	32	29	26
		9	32	27	23	31	26	23	29	25	22
		10	29	24	20	28	23	20	27	23	20

Fig. 1–5. Coefficient of utilization table.

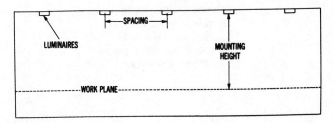

Fig. 1–6. For a given degree of uniformity, the larger the spacing-to-mounting height ratio, the fewer lighting fixtures required.

direction divided by projected area, as intercepted by the eye. Therefore, it is expressed as candelas per square inch in a certain direction. Candelas per square inch may be put into more convenient form by multiplying by 452 giving us luminance in "foot-lamberts." Another way of looking at luminance is in relation to illumination and reflection factor. For a non-specular surface

Luminance = illumination × reflection factor

$$L = E \times R$$

where

E = footcandles

R = reflection factor

L = footlamberts

To illustrate, if E = 100 footcandles and R = 50%, then L = 100 × .50 = 50 footlamberts.

The direct luminance or brightness of luminaires at various angles of view is a major factor in the visual comfort evaluation of an installation using those lighting fixtures. In general, it is desirable to minimize the brightness of ceiling-mounted fixtures at the high vertical angles, 60–90°. All units should be carefully examined for brightness values in footlamberts at angles affecting visual comfort. A typical published table is shown in Figure 1–7.

AVERAGE BRIGHTNESS DATA
Brightness in Footlamberts
Holophane No. 7100
2-F40CW Fluorescent Lamps
3100 Lumens Each

Vertical Angle	Across Axes	45° Plane	Along Axes
60	600	505	415
65	470	440	350
70	425	425	365
75	415	435	360
80	405	460	440
85	440	490	505

Fig. 1–7. Typical table giving brightness values in footlamberts at various angles.

Visual Comfort: Visual comfort describes the subjective response of people to the glare of a lighting system. Visual Comfort Probability (*VCP*) is a statistically based method which predicts percentage of people finding themselves comfortable when exposed to the worst glare position within a given, complete lighting installation. In addition to overall field brightness, VCP employs every known quantitative factor, such as lighting fixture luminance, size, and position, in its analysis. It therefore does not judge individual lighting units by isolated, single factors such as luminaire brightness, but in complete systems as they occur in actual use. While generally a laborious calculation for large rooms it has been greatly simplified and shortened by programming for computer use. Its greatest virtue lies in the opportunity it now affords the designer to compare system variations using one or any number of alternative lighting fixtures.

Distribution Curves: The photometric distribution curve—such as the one in Figure 1–8—is one of the lighting designers most valuable tools. It is a "map" of intensity (candelas) measured from many different directions. It is a two-dimensional representation and therefore shows data for one plane only. If, as is often the case, the distribution of the unit is symmetrical, the curve in one plane is sufficient for all calculations. If asymmetrical, such as with some types of street lighting and fluorescent units, two or more planes are required.

In general, indoor incandescent and mercury units are satisfied with a single vertical plane. Fluorescent lighting fixtures require a

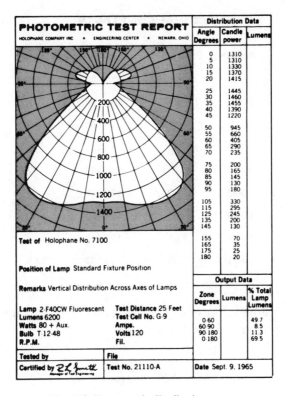

PHOTOMETRIC TEST REPORT

HOLOPHANE COMPANY INC • ENGINEERING CENTER • NEWARK, OHIO

Distribution Data		
Angle Degrees	Candle power	Lumens
0	1310	
5	1310	
10	1330	
15	1370	
20	1415	
25	1445	
30	1460	
35	1455	
40	1390	
45	1220	
50	945	
55	660	
60	405	
65	290	
70	235	
75	200	
80	165	
85	145	
90	130	
95	180	
105	330	
115	295	
125	245	
135	200	
145	130	
155	70	
165	35	
175	25	
180	20	

Test of Holophane No. 7100

Position of Lamp Standard Fixture Position

Remarks Vertical Distribution Across Axes of Lamps

Lamp 2-F40CW Fluorescent   **Test Distance** 25 Feet
Lumens 6200   **Test Cell No.** G-9
Watts 80 + Aux.   **Amps.**
Bulb T-12-48   **Volts** 120
R.P.M.   **Fil.**

Output Data		
Zone Degrees	Lumens	% Total Lamp Lumens
0-60		49.7
60-90		8.5
90-180		11.3
0-180		69.5

Tested by   **File**

Certified by R. L. Smith   **Test No.** 21110-A   **Date** Sept. 9, 1965

Fig. 1-8. Photometric distribution curve.

minimum of one plane along the lamp axis and one across the lamp axis. The greater the departure from symmetry, the more planes are needed for accurate calculations.

Bear in mind that photometric curves do not tell you directly how much light is being emitted in any given zone. However, this can be easily computed by the use of the table of zonal constants in Figure 1-9. Simply break the zone of interest, say 60-90° into smaller zones—such as 10° each. From the curve, read off the candlepower at the center of the zone. For the 60-70° zone, read candlepower at 65°, and so on. Multiply these candlepower readings by the table constant for that zone. For example, for zone 60-70°, the zonal constant is .99 and the candlepower is 290. Therefore, 290 × .99 = 287.1 lumens. Add the lumens in each zone to those of other zones and the result is the total lumens emitted from 60-90°.

ZONAL CONSTANTS

Zone (Degrees)	Zonal Constant	Zone (Degrees)	Zonal Constant
0-10	.10	170-180	.10
10-20	.28	160-170	.28
20-30	.46	150-160	.46
30-40	.63	140-150	.63
40-50	.77	130-140	.77
50-60	.90	120-130	.90
60-70	.99	110-120	.99
70-80	1.06	100-110	1.06
80-90	1.09	90-100	1.09

Fig. 1-9. Table of zonal constants.

How the values of intensity are determined is best understood by looking at the formula for illumination.

$$E(fc) = \frac{I}{D^2}$$

and therefore, $I = ED^2$. If we picture a lighting fixture located in the center of a large transparent sphere ruled into circles of latitude and longitude, we can then visualize a footcandle meter pressed against its surface, on which we read illumination at selected points. Putting the footcandle readings into the equation—along with the distance of the unit to the meter (the radius of the sphere)—we can calculate intensity at any point in space.

Intensity must be measured at a distance from the source that is large compared to the source dimensions and is a constant value. The actual requirement is that the measuring distance be at least five times the maximum dimension of the source. When measured in this way, intensity in a given direction, at any point in space, is constant.

Intensity distribution curves (photometric curves) are used to compute illumination levels, either by the inverse square formula, which gives the lighting level at a particular point, or in developing utilization coefficients for determining average footcandle levels over a general area. They are also valuable in figuring how much light is being generated by a luminaire.

Illumination Depreciation: Depreciation of illumination level results from aging of the lamps as well as dirt accumulation on and in the lighting fixtures and on the reflecting walls and ceilings of the

					Mult. Factor Lamp Deprec.	
Nominal lamp watts	ASA	Bulb Shape	Initial Lumens	Arc Center Length	Vert.	Horiz.
100	H38-4JA/C	BT-25	4100	5	.75	.74
100	H38-4HT	BT-25	4100	5	.79	.78
100	H38-4MP/C	A-23	3350	5⅞	.84	
175	H39-22KC/C	BT-28	7850	5	.91	.90
250	H37-5KC/C	BT-28	11850	5	.89	.85
250	H37-5KB	BT-28	12000	5	.91	.88
400	H33-1-GL/C	BT-37	20500	7	.89	.85
400	H33-1-CD	BT-37	20500	7	.91	.87
1000	H34-12GW/C	BT-56	55000	9½	.84	.79
1000	H34-12GV	BT-56	55000	9½	.85	.81
1000	H36-15GW/C	BT-56	57500	9½	.86	.81
1000	H36-15GV	BT-56	57500	9½	.88	.85

Mercury:

Dust and Dirt Depreciation on Luminaires.
(12 month depreciation.)

Room Condition	Direct	Semi Direct
Clean	.93	.88
Average	.90	.82
Dirty	.86	.78

Fig. 1-10. Light depreciation tables.

Fluorescent:

Nominal lamp watts	Type	Description	Approx. Initial Lumens	Mult. Factor Lamp Deprec.
20	F20T12	Preheat Fluorescent (Trigger Start)	1220	.85
40	F40CW	Preheat Rapid Start	3200	.92

Incandescent (Clear or I.F.)

Lamp Watts	Bulb Shape	Approx. Initial Lumens	L. C. Length	Mult. Factor Lamp Deprec.
60	A19	855	3⅛	.95
100	A21	1670	3⅞	.95
150	A23	2700	4⅝	.93
189	PS25	2900	5¼	.86
200	A23	3940	4⅝	.92
300 (med.)	PS30	6000	7	.88
300 (mog.)	PS35	5750	7	.90
500	PS40	9900	9½	.91
750 (mog.)	PS52	16700	9½	.93
1000	PS52	23300	9½	.93
1500	PS52	33000	9½	.84
Q250 MC	T4	4260		.97

Fig. 1–10. (*cont'd*)

area. Therefore, the calculation of average illumination levels must be calculated throughout the life of the installation.

Tables of depreciation for lamps and lighting fixtures are shown in Figure 1-10 and provide multiplying factors to be used with the IES Zonal Cavity Method. Two such factors are given for mercury lamps. This is important because most mercury lamps have a higher output over their lives when they are installed vertically than do those allowed to function horizontally. This can be an important factor in outdoor lighting.

ILLUMINATION LEVELS

The following illumination levels are the minimum recommended values as published by IES in the *Lighting Handbook*. They are merely a guide for use by lighting designers. Absolute values cannot and should not be assigned to cover all situations. Installation circumstances may alter these values and so the final discretion rests with the designer.

INDUSTRIAL

	Footcandles
Aircraft Manufacturing	
Stock parts	
Production	100
Inspection	200
Parts manufacturing	
Drilling, riveting, and screw fastening	70
Spray booths	100
Aircraft Hangars	
Repair service only	100
Automobile Manufacturing	
Frame assembly	50
Chassis assembly line	100
Final assembly and inspection line	200
Bakeries	
Mixing room	50
Wrapping room	30
Breweries	
Brew house	30
Filling (bottles, cans, and kegs)	50
Candy Making	
Chocolate department	50
Hand decorating	100
Canning and Preserving	
Initial grading raw material samples	50
Canning	100
Inspection	200
Central Station Indoor Locations	
Boiler platforms	10
Burner platform	20
Coal, conveyor, crusher, feeder, scale areas, pulverizer, fan area, and transfer tower	10

Fig. 1-11. Recommended illumination levels.

Control rooms
   Vertical face of switchboards
      Large   50
      Ordinary   30
   Bench boards (horizontal level)   50
  Turbine room   30
Central Station Outdoor Locations
   Catwalks   2
   Entrances, generating or service building
      (a) Main   10
      (b) Secondary   2
   Substation
      (a) General horizontal   2
      (b) Specific vertical (on disconnects)   2
Chemical Works
   Tanks for cooking, extractors, percolators, nitrators,
      and electrolytic cells   30
Clay Products and Cements
   Grinding, filter presses, and kiln rooms   30
   Enameling, color and glazing   100
Cloth Products
   Cloth inspection   2000
   Cutting   300
Dairy Products
   Filling inspection   100
   Pasteurizers and storage refrigerator   30
   Scales   70
Electrical Equipment Manufacturing
   Impregnating   50
   Insulating
      Coil winding and testing   100
Exterior Areas
   Entrances
      Active (pedestrian and/or conveyance)   5
      Inactive (normally locked, infrequently used)   1
   Storage areas
      Active   20
      Inactive   1
   Loading and unloading platforms   20
Flour Mills
   Rolling, sifting, and purifying   50
   Packing   30
Forge Shops   50

Fig. 1-11. (cont'd)

Foundries
    Annealing (furnaces)   30
    Core making
        Fine   100
        Medium   50
    Inspection
        Fine   500
        Medium   100
    Pouring   50
Garages—Automobile and Truck
    Repairs   100
    Storage   5
Glove Manufacturing
    Knitting   100
    Sewing and inspection   500
Iron and Steel Manufacturing
    Open hearth
        Stock yard   10
        Charging floor   20
        Hot top   30
        Stripping yard   20
        Skull cracker   10
    Rolling mills
        Blooming, slabbing, hot strip, and hot sheet   30
        Cold strip, plate   30
        Pipe, rod, tube, and wire drawing   50
    Tin plate mills
        Tinning and galvanizing   50
    Inspection
        Blackplate, bloom, and billet chipping   100
Laundries
    Washing   30
    Flatwork ironing, weighing, listing and marking   50
    Machine and press finishing and sorting   70
Leather Manufacturing
    Cleaning, tanning, and stretching, and vats   30
    Finishing and scarfing   100
Locker Rooms   20
Machine Shops
    Rough bench and machine work   50
    Medium bench and machine work   100
    Fine bench and machine work   500
Materials Handling
    Wrapping, packing, and labeling   50

Fig. 1–11. (*cont'd*)

Loading and trucking	20
Picking, stock, and classifying	30
Meat Packing	
Slaughtering	30
Cleaning, cutting, cooking, grinding, canning, and packing	100
Paint Shops	
Dipping, simple spraying, and firing	50
Rubbing, ordinary hand painting, and finishing art	50
Fine hand painting and finishing	100
Paper Manufacturing	
Beaters, grinding, and calendering	30
Finishing, cutting, trimming, and paper-making machines	50
Hand counting, wet end of paper machine	70
Paper machine reel, paper inspection, and laboratories	100
Rewinder	150
Printing Industries	
Type foundries	
Matrix making, dressing type	100
Printing plants	
Color inspection and appraisal	200
Composing room	100
Presses	70
Proofreading	150
Electrotyping	100
Photo engraving	
Etching, staging, and blocking	50
Routing, finishing, proofing, tint laying, and masking	100
Rubber Tire and Tube Manufacturing	
Banbury, plasticating, and milling	30
Calendering	50
Tire Building	
Solid tire	30
Pneumatic tire	50
Curing department	70
Final inspection	
Tube casing	200
Sheet Metal Works	
Presses, shears, stamps, spinning, and medium bench work	50
Scribing	200
Ship Yards	
General	5

Fig. 1–11. (*cont'd*)

Ways	10
Fabrication areas	30
Shoe Manufacturing	
Cutting and stitching	300
Stairways, Washrooms and Other Service Areas	20
Storage Rooms or Warehouses	
Rough bulky	10
Medium	20
Fine	50
Tobacco Products	
Drying, stripping, and general	30
Grading and sorting	200
Welding	
General illumination	50
Precision manual arc welding	1000
Woodworking	
Rough sawing and bench work	30
Sizing, planing, rough sanding, medium machine and bench work, gluing, veneering, and cooperage	50
Fine bench and machine work and fine sanding and finishing	100

INSTITUTIONAL

Art Galleries	
General	30
On statuary and other displays	100
Churches	
Altar, ark, and reredos	100
Choir and chancel	30
Classrooms	30
Main worship area	15
Hospitals	
Autopsy room	100
Morgue, general	20
Corridor	
General	20
Operating and delivery suites and laboratories	30
Examination and treatment room	
General	50
Examining table	100
Exits, at floor	5

Fig. 1-11 (*cont'd*)

Fracture room	
General	50
Fracture table	200
Kitchen	70
Dishwashing	30
Laboratories	
Work tables	50
Close work	100
Lobby	30
Nurses' station	
General, day	70
General, night	30
Desk and charts	70
Parking lot	1
Private rooms and wards	
General	10
Reading	30
Stairways	20
Surgery	
Instrument and sterile supply room	30
Clean-up room (instruments)	100
Scrub-up room	30
Operating room, general	100
Operating table	2500
Waiting room	
General	20
Reading	30
Hotels	
Auditoriums	
Assembly only	15
Exhibitions	30
Dancing	5
Entrance foyer	30
Lobby	
General lighting	10
Reading and working areas	30
Schools	
Reading printed material	30
Reading pencil writing	70
Drafting and benchwork	100
Auditoriums (assembly only)	15
Swimming pools, indoor	30
Swimming pools, outdoor	10
Libraries	70
Laboratories	100

Fig. 1–11. (*cont'd*)

COMMERCIAL

Banks	
Lobby	
General	50
Writing areas	70
Tellers' stations, posting and keypunch	150
Offices	
Designing and detailed drafting	200
Accounting, auditing, bookkeeping, and	
business machine operation	150
Regular office work	100
Stores	
Circulation areas	30
Merchandising areas	
Service	100
Self-service	200
Stockrooms	30

Fig. 1-11 (*cont'd*)

ELECTRICAL WIRING SYMBOLS

The purpose of lighting drawing, as related to construction projects, is to show the complete design and layout of the lighting system. In preparing such drawings, the lighting layout is shown through the use of lines, symbols, and notation which should indicate, beyond any doubt, exactly what is required.

Many engineers, designers, and draftsmen use symbols adapted by the America National Standards Institute (ANSI). However, no definite standard schedule of symbols is always used in its entirety. Consulting engineering firms quite frequently modify these standard symbols to meet their own needs. In order to identify the symbols properly, on one of the drawings or in the written specifications the engineer provides a list of symbols with a descriptive note for each, clearly indicating the part of the wiring system which the symbol represents.

Figure 1-12 shows a list of electrical reference symbols which have been modified for use by one consulting engineering firm. In this list, it is evident that many of the symbols are the same basic form, but, because of some slight difference, their meaning changes. For example, five of the incandescent lighting fixtures have the same basic form—a circle—but the addition of a line, shading, etc., gives

ELECTRICAL SYMBOLS

SWITCH OUTLETS

Single-Pole Switch	S
Double-Pole Switch	S_2
Three-Way Switch	S_3
Four-Way Switch	S_4
Key-Operated Switch	S_K
Switch and Fusestat Holder	S_FH
Switch and Pilot Lamp	S_P
Fan Switch	S_F
Switch for Low-Voltage Switching System	S_L
Master Switch for Low-Voltage Switching System	S_{LM}
Switch and Single Receptacle	⊖S
Switch and Duplex Receptacle	⊜S
Door Switch	S_D
Time Switch	S_T
Momentary Contact Switch	S_{MC}
Ceiling Pull Switch	Ⓢ
"Hand-Off-Auto" Control Switch	HOA
Multi-Speed Control Switch	M
Push Button	•

RECEPTACLE OUTLETS

Where weather proof, explosion proof, or other specific types of devices are to be required, use the upper-case subscript letters. For example, weather proof single or duplex receptacles would have the uppercase WP subscript letters noted alongside of the symbol. All outlets should be grounded.

Single Receptacle Outlet	⊖
Duplex Receptacle Outlet	⊜
Triplex Receptacle Outlet	⊕
Quadruplex Receptacle Outlet	⊕
Duplex Receptacle Outlet-Split Wired	⊖
Triplex Receptacle Outlet-Split Wired	⊕

250 Volt Receptable Single Phase Use Subscript Letter to Indicate Function (DW-Dishwasher; RA-Range, CD - Clothes Dryer) or numeral (with explanation in symbol schedule)

250 Volt Receptacle Three Phase	⊜
Clock Receptacle	Ⓒ
Fan Receptacle	Ⓕ
Floor Single Receptacle Outlet	⊟
Floor Duplex Receptacle Outlet	⊟
Floor Special-Purpose Outlet	⬡ *
Floor Telephone Outlet - Public	◀
Floor Telephone Outlet - Private	◁

Example of the use of several floor outlet symbols to identify a 2, 3, or more gang floor outlet:

⊖◀◁ ,

Underfloor Duct and Junction Box for Triple, Double or Single Duct System as indicated by the number of parallel lines.

Example of use of various symbols to identify location of different types of outlets or connections for underfloor duct or cellular floor systems:

Cellular Floor Header Duct

_____

*Use numeral keyed to explanation in drawing list of symbols to indicate usage.

Fig. 1–12. Electrical reference symbols.

CIRCUITING

Wiring Exposed (not in conduit) ——E——

Wiring Concealed In Ceiling or Wall ————

Wiring Concealed in Floor — — — —

Wiring Existing* - - - - - - - -

Wiring Turned Up ————o

Wiring Turned Down ————●

Branch Circuit Home Run to Panel Board. 2 1

Number of arrows indicates number of circuits. (A number at each arrow may be used to identify circuit number.)**

BUS DUCTS AND WIREWAYS

Trolley Duct*** | T | | T |

Busway (Service, Feeder, or (Plug-in)*** | B | | B |

Cable Trough Ladder or Channel*** | C | | C |

Wireway*** | W | | W |

PANELBOARDS, SWITCHBOARDS AND RELATED EQUIPMENT

Flush Mounted Panelboard and Cabinet***

Surface Mounted Panelboard and Cabinet***

Switchboard, Power Control Center, Unit Substations (Should be drawn to scale)***

Flush Mounted Terminal Cabinet (In small scale drawings the TC may be indicated alongside the symbol)***   TC

Surface Mounted Terminal Cabinet (In small scale drawings the TC may be indicated alongside the symbol)***   TC

Pull Box (Identify in relation to Wiring System Section and Size)

Motor or Other Power Controller (May be a starter or contactor)***

Externally Operated Disconnection Switch***

Combination Controller and Disconnection Means***

POWER EQUIPMENT

Electric Motor (HP as indicated)   ¼

Power Transformer

Pothead (Cable Termination)

Circuit Element, e.g., Circuit Breaker   CB

Circuit Breaker

Fusible Element

Single-Throw Knife Switch

Double-Throw Knife Switch

Ground   —||

Battery   —|⊢

Contactor   C

Photoelectric Cell   PE

Voltage Cycles, Phase   Ex: 480/60/3

Relay   R

Equipment (Connection (as noted)   ●

*Note: Use heavy-weight line to identify service and feeders. Indicate empty conduit by notation CO (conduit only).
**Note: Any circuit without further identification indicates two-wire circuit. For a greater number of wires, indicate with cross lines, e.g.:

—|||— 3 wires;   —||||— 4 wires, etc.

Neutral wire may be shown longer. Unless indicated otherwise, the wire size of the circuit is the minimum size required by the specification. Identify different functions, of wiring system. e.g., signalling system by notation or other means.
***Identify by Notation or Schedule

Fig. 1–12. (cont'd)

each an individual meaning. A good procedure to follow in learning symbols is to first learn the basic form and then apply the variations for obtaining different meanings.

LUMINAIRE DATA

A luminaire is a complete lighting unit—lamp, sockets, and equipment for controlling light, such as reflectors and diffusers. On electric discharge lighting, the luminaire also includes a ballast. The common term used for luminaire is *lighting fixture*, or in some cases, just *fixture*.

Luminance given off by a lighting fixture is controlled by several methods so that proper light distribution and comfort are obtained. For example, the lens controls high-angle luminance where a specific light distribution light pattern is desired, diffusers are used where general diffusion of light is desired, shielding—in the form of louvers, baffles, and reflectors—is used to reduce glare and excessive brightness, and reflectors can be used to direct light in useful directions.

A lighting fixture may be classified by its distribution of light, type of lamp used, or description. The distribution of light is based on the percentage of lumens emitted above and below the horizontal.

Direct—0 to 10 Percent

Down 90–100%. This type is most efficient from the standpoint of getting the maximum amount of light from the source to the working plane. On the other hand, this type may produce greatest luminance differences between ceiling and luminaire, and may also produce greatest shadows and glare.

Semidirect—10 to 40 Percent Up

Down 60–90%. Most of the light is still down, but some is directed up to the ceiling.

General Diffuse—40 to 60 Percent Down

Up 40–60%. This type makes light about equally available in all directions. A modification of the general diffuse is the Direct-Indirect, which is shielded to emit little light in the zone near the horizontal.

Semi-Indirect—60 to 90 Percent Up

Down 10–40%. Here the greater percentage of the light is directed toward the ceiling and upper walls. The ceiling should be of high reflectance in order to reflect the light.

Indirect—90 to 100 Percent Up

Down 0–10%. Totally indirect reflectors direct all of the light up to the ceiling. Some types are slightly luminous to offset the luminance difference between the luminaire and the bright ceiling. Shadows are at a minimum, although glare may be present due to a bright ceiling. Inside-frosted lamps should be used instead of clear-glass incandescent lamps to prevent streaks and striations on the ceiling. Low-luminance fluorescent lamps are recommended.

The classification of fixture according to source will be either incandescent, fluorescent, or high-intensity discharge lighting, all of which were described previously. Applications will include industrial, commercial, institutional, residential, and special-purpose applications such as for duct-tight, vapor-tight, and explosion-proof areas.

Examples of several types of lighting fixtures are shown in Figure 1–13. Note that light distribution curves, maximum spacing, and coefficients of utilization are given. These values are needed for lighting calculations and for selection of design and layout of lighting systems for all types of areas.

LIGHT SOURCES

The primary purpose of a light source is the production of light, and the efficiency with which a lamp fulfills this purpose is expressed in terms of lumens emitted per watt of power consumed—*luminous efficacy*. If a light source could be developed that would radiate all the energy it received as visible light, it would produce approximately 680 lumens per watt of power consumed. Since all practical light sources produce considerable quantities of infrared, and since there is some inevitable energy loss by conduction and convection, no lamp closely approaches the theoretical maximum efficacy. However, reference to earlier products of lamp manufacture shows the progress

DAY-BRITE OCTET® 7
SECTION 10 SHEET 65A

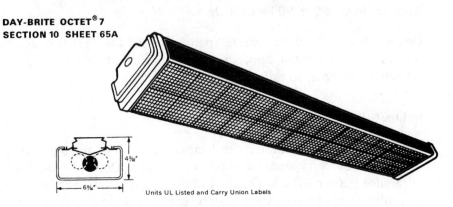

Units UL Listed and Carry Union Labels

ENGINEERING DATA

ROOM SIZE	30 FOOTCANDLES			50 FOOTCANDLES		
	1-Lamp Units	1-Lamp Cont. Row	2-Lamp Units	1-Lamp Cont. Row	2-Lamp Units	2-Lamp Cont. Row
SMALL	5' x 5'	6-ft.	6' x 8'	4-ft.	5' x 6'	7-ft.
MEDIUM	6' x 6'	9-ft.	6' x 10'	5-ft.	6' x 6'	9-ft.
LARGE	6' x 8'	12-ft.	7' x 10'	7-ft.	5' x 8'	10-ft.

FIXTURE SPACING, 40-WATT RAPID-START

70 FOOTCANDLES	100 FOOTCANDLES
2-Lamp Cont. Row	2-Lamp Cont. Row
5-ft.	3-ft.
6-ft.	4-ft.
7-ft.	5-ft.

NOTE: Should not exceed recommended SPACING-MOUNTING RATIOS shown. Footcandles are average maintained

TWO LAMP OCTET-7

EFFECTIVE FLOOR CAVITY REFLECTANCE—20% pfc

EFFECTIVE CEILING CAVITY REFLECTANCE pcc		80%			50%			10%		
% WALL REFLECTANCE pw		50%	30%	10%	50%	30%	10%	50%	30%	10%
	1	.70	.67	.64	.61	.58	.56	.50	.48	.47
	2	.61	.56	.52	.53	.49	.46	.44	.41	.39
	3	.54	.48	.43	.47	.42	.39	.39	.36	.33
	4	.48	.42	.37	.42	.37	.33	.35	.32	.29
	5	.42	.36	.31	.37	.32	.28	.31	.28	.25
	6	.38	.32	.27	.34	.29	.25	.28	.25	.22
	7	.34	.28	.24	.30	.25	.22	.26	.22	.19
	8	.31	.25	.20	.27	.22	.19	.23	.20	.17
	9	.29	.23	.18	.25	.20	.17	.21	.17	.15
	10	.28	.21	.17	.24	.18	.15	.20	.16	.13

NADIR C.P.-1120
3100 LUMEN LAMPS
•
MAINTENANCE FACTORS
Good .75   Med. .70
Poor .65
•
Average Brightness in the 60°-90° zone from Nadir shall not exceed 875 Footlamberts endwise or 1700 Footlamberts crosswise.

ROOM CAVITY RATIOS

MAXIMUM SPACING TO MOUNTING HEIGHT RATIO ABOVE WORK PLANE 1:35

(A)

Fig. 1–13. Several types of lighting fixtures. (A, B, C, D)

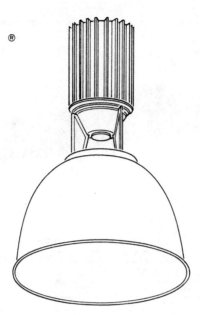

COEFFICIENTS OF UTILIZATION

ZONAL CAVITY METHOD

			SINGLE									
EFFECTIVE FLOOR *pfc*						20%						
EFFECTIVE CEILING *pcc*				80%			50%			10%		0%
% WALL REFLECTANCE *pw*			50%	30%	10%	50%	30%	10%	50%	30%	10%	0%
NADIR C.P.-6440 21,000 LUMEN COLOR-IMPROVED LAMPS • MAINTENANCE FACTORS Good .80 Med. .70 Poor .60	ROOM CAVITY RATIOS	1	.86	.83	.80	.76	.75	.73	.66	.65	.64	.61
		2	.77	.72	.68	.69	.66	.63	.60	.58	.56	.54
		3	.69	.63	.59	.62	.58	.55	.55	.52	.50	.48
		4	.62	.56	.51	.56	.52	.48	.50	.47	.44	.42
		5	.56	.49	.45	.51	.46	.42	.45	.42	.39	.37
		6	.50	.44	.39	.46	.41	.37	.41	.37	.34	.33
		7	.46	.39	.35	.42	.37	.33	.37	.34	.31	.29
		8	.41	.34	.30	.38	.32	.29	.34	.30	.27	.25
		9	.37	.30	.26	.34	.29	.25	.30	.26	.23	.22
		10	.34	.27	.23	.31	.26	.22	.26	.23	.21	.19

MAXIMUM SPACING TO MOUNTING HEIGHT RATIO (ABOVE WORK PLANE): 1.3

Fig. 1–13B.

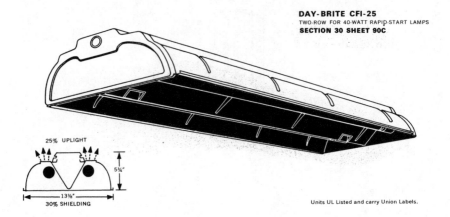

DAY-BRITE CFI-25
TWO-ROW FOR 40-WATT RAPID-START LAMPS
SECTION 30 SHEET 90C

25% UPLIGHT

5¾"

13⅜"

30% SHIELDING

Units UL Listed and carry Union Labels.

ENGINEERING DATA

ROOM SIZE	FIXTURE SPACING CFI-25, 4-FOOT RAPID-START		
	50 FOOTCANDLES		70 FOOTCANDLES
	SINGLE 8-FOOT TANDEM UNITS	CONTINUOUS RUNS	CONTINUOUS RUNS
SMALL	9 x 9	10-ft.	7-ft.
MEDIUM	10 x 10	12-ft.	9-ft.
LARGE	11 x 11	15-ft.	11-ft.

100 FOOTCANDLES	150 FOOTCANDLES
CONTINUOUS RUNS	CONTINUOUS RUNS
5-ft.	—
6-ft.	4-ft.
8-ft.	5-ft.

NOTE: Should not exceed recommended SPACING-MOUNTING RATIOS.
Footcandles are average maintained values.

COEFFICIENTS OF UTILIZATION

		EFFECTIVE FLOOR CAVITY REFLECTANCE—20% *pfc*									
EFFECTIVE CEILING CAVITY REFLECTANCE *pcc*		80%			50%			10%			0%
% WALL REFLECTANCE *pw*		50%	30%	10%	50%	30%	10%	50%	30%	10%	0%
	1	.87	.84	.81	.75	.3	.71	.62	.60	.59	.56
NADIR C.P.-1490 3100 LUMEN LAMPS	2	.77	.72	.68	.67	.63	.0	.55	.53	.51	.48
	3	.68	.62	.5	.60	.55	.52	50	.47	.44	.42
MAINTENANCE FACTORS Good .75 Med. .70 Poor .65	4	.61	.54	.49	.54	.48	.45	.5	.41	.39	.36
	5	.54	.47	.42	.48	.42	.38	.40	.36	.33	.31
	6	.48	.41	.36	.43	.37	.33	.36	.32	.29	.27
Average Brightness in the 60°-90° zone from Nadir shall not exceed 1110 Footlamberts endwise or 440 Footlamberts crosswise.	7	.44	.36	.31	.38	.33	.29	.3	.28	.25	.23
	8	.39	.32	.7	.34	.29	.25	.29	.25	.22	.20
	9	.35	.28	.23	.31	.25	.22	.26	.22	.19	.17
	10	.32	.25	.20	.28	.22	.19	.24	.20	.17	.15

ROOM CAVITY RATIOS

MAXIMUM RECOMMENDED SPACING TO MOUNTING HEIGHT RATIO ABOVE WORK PLANE IS: 1.30
ZONAL-CAVITY METHOD.

Fig. 1–13C

TABLES OF FIXTURE EFFICIENCIES AND C.U.'S WITH STANDARD LENS AND TYPICAL OPTIONAL DIFFUSERS
COEFFICIENTS OF UTILIZATION – ZONAL-FACTOR INTERFLECTANCE METHOD
PHOTOMETRIC REPORTS BY INDEPENDENT TESTING LABORATORIES, INC., BOULDER, COLORADO 80302

1208,1209 With Standard Kirlin Lens

EFFICIENCY 65.6% — WATTS 150 — LAMP A-21 — 2760 Lumens — S/MH 0.9

ZONE	LUMENS	% LAMP	% FIXT
0°–30°	740	26.8	40.9
0°–40°	1092	38.6	60.3
0°–60°	1603	58.1	86.5
0°–90°	1811	65.6	100.0

RW	50	30
J 0.6	37	33
I 0.8	45	39
H 1.0	50	45
G 1.25	55	50
F 1.5	59	54
E 2.0	64	60
D 2.5	68	64
C 3.0	70	66
B 4.0	74	70
A 5.0	76	72

1208,1209 With Concave Kirlin Lens

EFFICIENCY 59.5% — WATTS 150 — LAMP A-21 — 2760 Lumens — S/MH 0.9

ZONE	LUMENS	% LAMP	% FIXT
0°–30°	875	31.7	53.3
0°–40°	1205	43.6	73.4
0°–60°	1530	56.4	93.2
0°–90°	1641	59.5	100.0

RW	50	30
J 0.6	39	36
I 0.8	46	42
H 1.0	50	46
G 1.25	54	50
F 1.5	57	52
E 2.0	61	57
D 2.5	64	60
C 3.0	66	62
B 4.0	68	65
A 5.0	70	67

1208-11,1209-11 With Option -11 Concentrating Lens

EFFICIENCY 68.9% — WATTS 150 — LAMP A-21 — 2760 Lumens — S/MH 0.8

ZONE	LUMENS	% LAMP	% FIXT
0°–30°	807	29.2	42.5
0°–40°	1166	42.2	61.3
0°–60°	1696	61.5	83.3
0°–90°	1900	68.9	100.0

RW	50	30
J 0.6	39	35
I 0.8	47	42
H 1.0	53	49
G 1.25	58	53
F 1.5	62	57
E 2.0	68	63
D 2.5	71	66
C 3.0	74	70
B 4.0	77	74
A 5.0	80	76

1208-13,1209-13 With Option -13 Dished Lens

EFFICIENCY 63.2% — WATTS 150 — LAMP A-21 — 2760 Lumens — S/MH 0.6

ZONE	LUMENS	% LAMP	% FIXT
0°–30°	776	28.1	44.5
0°–40°	1025	37.1	58.8
0°–60°	1423	51.5	81.6
0°–90°	1706	61.8	97.8

RW	50	30
J 0.6	34	31
I 0.8	41	36
H 1.0	46	41
G 1.25	51	45
F 1.5	54	49
E 2.0	59	54
D 2.5	63	58
C 3.0	65	61
B 4.0	69	65
A 5.0	71	67

1208-14,1209-14 With Option -14 Anopal Bowl

EFFICIENCY 53.6% — WATTS 150 — LAMP A-21 — 2760 Lumens — S/MH 1.3

ZONE	LUMENS	% LAMP	% FIXT
0°–30°	336	12.2	23.7
0°–40°	567	20.2	37.7
0°–60°	1019	36.9	68.9
0°–90°	1404	50.9	95.0

RW	50	30
J 0.6	22	18
I 0.8	28	23
H 1.0	32	27
G 1.25	36	31
F 1.5	40	35
E 2.0	45	40
D 2.5	48	43
C 3.0	51	46
B 4.0	54	50
A 5.0	56	53

Fig. 1-13D.

that has been made. The efficacy of the 60–watt incandescent filament lamp, for example, has been increased three and one-half times
during the past 45 years by changing from carbon to tungsten as a
filament material, from vacuum to gas-filled construction, and from
straight filament wire to coiled and then coiled coil filaments.

However, the incandescent filament lamp has certain characteristics which make it inherently inefficient as a source of light, and
although it is probable that efficacies will still be raised slightly by
further refinements in manufacturing processes, the maximum
possible values have already been approached. The electric discharge
lamp produces light by an entirely different process, and is capable
of achieving much higher efficacies. Clear mercury lamps have
efficacies up to 57 lumens per watt, mercury-fluorescent lamps up to
62. A number of fluorescent lamps now provide over 70 lumens per
watt, and some provide over 80. Continued development work will
undoubtedly lead to further improvements and still higher outputs.

A third method of producing light is electroluminescence, in which
light is generated in a solid material by the direct application of an
alternating electric field. No filament, gaseous vapor, or enclosing
bulb is used, and light is produced in a film a few thousandths of an
inch thick. A typical electroluminescent source consists of a thin
layer of phosphor between two conducting plates, one of which is
transparent. Luminance depends on the voltage and frequency of the
supply, as well as on the chemical composition of the phosphor.

Filament Lamps

The filament lamp produces light by virtue of a wire or filament
heated to incandescence by the flow of electric current through it.
Chapter 2 describes the principal parts and operation of typical filament lamps.

The sizes and shapes of lamp bulbs are designated by a letter or
letters followed by a number. The letters indicate the shape of the
bulb: S = Straight Side, F = Flame, G = Round or Globular, T =
Tubular, PS = Pear Straight Neck, PAR = Parabolic, R = Reflector,
A = Arbitrary Designation applied to the bulbs commonly used for
general lighting service lamps of 200 watts or less. The number in a
bulb designation indicates the diameter of the bulb in eighths of an

inch. For example, "T–10" indicates a tubular bulb having a diameter of 10/8 or 1¼ inches (Figure 1–14).

Bulb size and shape are determined by the purpose for which the lamp is to be used. Obviously the larger the bulb, the greater the area over which tungsten vaporized from the filament will be distributed as the lamp ages and gradually blackens. The thinner this deposit, the less light it absorbs, and the better the light output of the lamp throughout life. From the standpoint of lighting equipment cost, there is a limit to desirable bulb size, and the size of a general lighting service lamp is usually a compromise between performance and economic considerations. In projection lamps and certain other types where minimum size outweighs maintenance of light output, bulbs often are smaller than those for general lighting service lamps of equal wattage ratings.

To diffuse the light from the filament, many lamps have inside frosted bulbs produced by a light acid etching applied to the inner surface of the bulb. Some types of lamps are available with an inside white silica coating which provides still greater diffusion. The inside frosted bulb absorbs no measurable amount of light, whereas the silica coating absorbs about two percent. With both treatments, the outer surface of the bulb is left smooth and easily cleaned. Diffusing bulbs are preferred for most general lighting purposes, but where accurate control of light is involved, as in optical systems, clear bulb lamps are necessary.

Other finishes applied to some general lighting service lamps are white bowl and silvered bowl. A white bowl lamp has a translucent white coating on the inner surface of the bulb bowl; this coating reduces both direct and reflected glare from open fixtures. A silvered bowl lamp has an opaque silver coating applied to the bowl. The inner

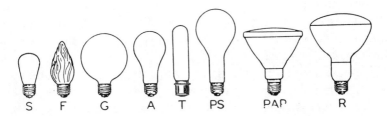

Fig. 1–14. Various shapes of filament lamps available today.

surface of this coating is a highly specular reflector which is not affected by dust or deterioration, and therefore remains efficient throughout the life of the lamp. Silvered bowl lamps are commonly used in certain types of equipment for totally indirect lighting, and also occasionally in direct fixtures such as standard dome reflectors.

Colored light in filament lamps is produced subtractively by a bulb that absorbs light of colors other than those desired. For example, a red bulb will absorb green and white, but will not absorb red. Most colored bulbs are made by applying a pigmented coating to either the inner or the outer surface of a clear bulb, or by fusing an enamel into the outer surface (ceramic coating). The most commonly used colors are red, blue, green, yellow, orange, ivory, flametint, and white.

Lamps with slightly colored inside silica coating in pink (Beauty Tone lamps) are available in the 3–way most commonly used in residence lighting equipment. They are used where delicately tinted light is desired for decorative effect. Ceramic coatings and inside coatings are satisfactory for either outdoor or indoor use, but most outside coatings are not permanent and are recommended for use only where they are protected from the weather.

Another type of colored lamp has a bulb of natural colored glass, made by adding chemicals to the ingredients of the glass. Natural colored bulbs are made in daylight blue, blue, amber, green, and ruby. They produce purer colors than do coated bulbs, and are often used for theatrical and photographic lighting. For decorative or display lighting, coated lamps are preferred over natural colored lamps because of their lower cost.

The most widely used natural colored lamp is the daylight blue. Because the daylight blue bulb reduces the amount of red and yellow light common to incandescent lamps, the light produced resembles daylight more than does any other lamp. Since this is accomplished with increased lamp cost and with some 35% less absorption in light, daylight blue lamps should be used only where the lighting requirements make it necessary.

The base provides a means of connecting the lamp bulb to the socket. For general lighting purposes, screw-type bases are most commonly used. Most general-lighting-service lamps (300 watts and below) have medium screw bases. The higher wattages (three hundred watts and above) use the mogul screw base. Some of the lower-wattage lamps, particularly the sign, indicator, and decorative types, are made with candelabra or intermediate screw bases (Figure 1–15).

A light source (lamp filament) cannot be accurately aligned with respect to an optical system by means of a screw base. Filament orientation is provided by a number of other types of bases, the most common of which are the prefocus, bipost, bayonet, and special pin-type bases for projection lamps. A bipost base, usually used on high-wattage lamps, consists of two metal pins or posts imbedded in a glass "cup" forming the end of the lamp bulb. Most screw and pre-focus bases are attached to the bulb by specially designed basing cement. Other bases used on certain lamps include prong types, screw terminals, contact lugs, flexible leads, recessed single contact, and a number of other types for specific applications.

The filament is the light-producing element of the lamp, and the primary considerations in its design are its electrical characteristics. The wattage of a filament lamp is equal to the voltage delivered at the socket times the amperes flowing through the filament. By Ohm's Law ($I = E/R$) the current (amperes) is determined by the voltage and the resistance, which in turn depends on the length and the diameter of the filament wire. The higher the wattage of a lamp of a given voltage, the higher the current and therefore the greater the diameter of the filament wire required to carry it. The higher the voltage of a lamp of a given wattage, the lower the current and the smaller the diameter of the filament wire (Figure 1–16).

The filament forms in common use today (Figure 1–17) are designated by a letter or letters indicating whether the wire is straight or coiled, a number specifying the general form of the filament, and

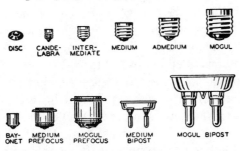

DISC   CANDE-LABRA   INTER-MEDIATE   MEDIUM   ADMEDIUM   MOGUL

BAY-ONET   MEDIUM PREFOCUS   MOGUL PREFOCUS   MEDIUM BIPOST   MOGUL BIPOST

Fig. 1–15. Types of incandescent lamp bases currently in use.

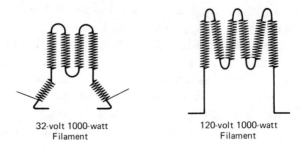

32-volt 1000-watt
Filament

120-volt 1000-watt
Filament

Fig. 1–16. Two 100–watt lamp filaments; note the larger coils (and thus higher resistance) for the 120–volt filament.

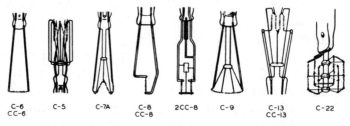

| C-6 | C-5 | C-7A | C-8 | 2CC-8 | C-9 | C-13 | C-22 |
| CC-6 | | | CC-8 | | | CC-13 | |

Fig. 1–17. Several types of lamp filaments currently in use.

sometimes another letter indicating arrangement of the supports. As the first letter of a filament designation, S means a straight (uncoiled) filament wire, C a coiled wire, CC a coiled coil, and R a flat or ribbon-shaped wire. The numbers and other letters assigned to the various filament forms are purely arbitrary.

Incandescent lamps were first made with evacuated bulbs, the purpose being merely to keep the filament from burning up by excluding oxygen. Later it was discovered that the pressure exerted on the filament by an inert gas introduced into the bulb retarded the evaporation of tungsten, thus making it possible to design lamps for higher filament temperatures. Vacuum lamps are now designated as "type B" lamps, gas-filled lamps as "type C".

The gas removes some heat from the filament, as a result of conduction and convection losses not present in the vacuum lamp. The larger the surface of the wire in proportion to its volume or mass, the greater this cooling effect becomes, until eventually it nullifies the gain achieved by using the filling gas. Filaments with a current rating of less than 1/3 ampere have a wire diameter so small that the introduction of gas is a disadvantage rather than an advantage. For this reason, standard-voltage general lighting service lamps of less than 40 watts are of the vacuum or type B construction, while lamps of 40 watts and higher are gas-filled.

Nitrogen and argon are the gases most commonly used in lamp manufacture. Projection lamps use an atmosphere of 100% nitrogen. Most other types have a mixture of nitrogen and argon, the proportions varying with the lamp and the service for which it is designed. High-voltage lamps, for example, are filled with approximately 50% argon and 50% nitrogen, the higher wattage standard-voltage types about 90% argon and 10% nitrogen, and the lower wattage standard-voltage types and all street series lamps about 98% argon and 2% nitrogen. Some nitrogen is necessary to prevent arcing across the lead-in wires, which would occur if pure argon were used. The greater the inherent tendency of a lamp to arc, the higher the percentage of nitrogen in its gas mixture.

Krypton is a relatively rare and expensive gas which has a higher atomic weight than either argon or nitrogen, and therefore causes less energy loss by conduction and convection. It is primarily used in certain miniature lamps such as miner's cap lamps, where the limited capacity of the battery power supply makes it essential to obtain the greatest possible efficiency. Hydrogen, because of its low atomic weight, is used in certain very special types of flashing signal lamps where rapid cooling of the filament is important. See the following table for the atomic weights of the gases most commonly used in lamps.

ATOMIC WEIGHTS OF GASES

Hydrogen	1.008
Nitrogen	14.008
Argon	39.944
Krypton	83.7

Operating characteristics and other pertinent information on other types of light sources (fluorescent, mercury, etc.) appear in chapters dealing with the respective light source.

Chapter 2

Lighting with Incandescent Lamps

Incandescent lamps are now made in thousands of different types and colors from a fraction of a watt to over 10 kilowatts each, and for practically any conceivable lighting application.

Regardless of the type or size, all incandescent filament lamps consist of a sealed glass envelope containing a filament. Light is produced when the filament is heated to incandescence (white light) by its resistance to a flow of electric current. Figure 2-1 illustrates the basic components of an incandescent lamp.

The quartz-iodine tungsten-filament lamp is basically an incandescent lamp, since light is produced from the incandescence of its coiled tungsten filament. However, the quartz lamp envelope is filled with an iodine vapor, which prevents the evaporation of the tungsten filament. This evaporation is what normally occurs in conventional incandescent lamps; then the bulb begins to blacken, light output deteriorates, and eventually the filament burns out. While the quartz-iodine lamp has approximately the same efficiency as an equivalent conventional incandescent lamp, it has the advantages of double the normal life, low lumen depreciation, and a smaller bulb for a given wattage. Figure 2-2 illustrates the basic components of a quartz-iodine lamp.

Some of the advantages of incandescent lamps are as follows:

- Relatively low initial installation cost.
- Not greatly affected by ambient temperatures.
- Direction easily controlled.
- Brightness easily controlled.
- High color quality.

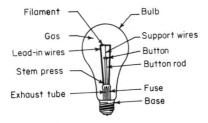

Fig. 2-1. Basic components of an incandescent lamp.

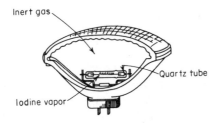

Fig. 2-2. Basic components of a quartz-iodine lamp.

Some of the disadvantages include:

- Less efficient than most electric-discharge lamps.
- Higher operating cost per lumen.
- More heat produced per lumen than with electric-discharge lighting, causing the need for a larger air-conditioning system, thus increasing energy consumption and operating cost.

With the exception of residential lighting, incandescent lamps should be installed only in areas where their use will be of short duration. Such areas may include clothes closets and small storage closets, janitors' closets, infrequently used storage areas, or places where the use of a more efficient light source would be impractical.

In selecting incandescent lamps, remember that higher-wattage general-service lamps are more efficient than lamps of a lower wattage. One 200-watt lamp, for example, produces about 4000 lumens as compared to 3500 lumens from two 100-watt lamps.

General-service incandescent lamps are more efficient than extended-service lamps, but have a shorter lamp life. Where the replacement of lamps causes no large problem, all incandescent lamps should be of the general-service type; hard-to-reach lighting fixtures, however, should be lamped with extended-service lamps.

The dimming of lights is another possibility in conserving energy when incandescent lamps are used as the main light source. In addition to helping to conserve energy, dimming systems are ideal for providing security lighting and allowing selective variation in illumination levels for other multifunction areas where the lighting needs cannot always be predicted.

PORCELAIN LAMP HOLDER

The porcelain lamp holder in Figure 2–3 is the simplest of all light fixtures and has been much used as a light source for unfinished areas in commercial and residential buildings. It is suitable for use in commerce and industry in small, seldom-used areas such as janitors' closets (Figure 2–4) and storage areas. Such fixtures are also used in garages, unfinished basements and attics, and in outbuildings in residential construction.

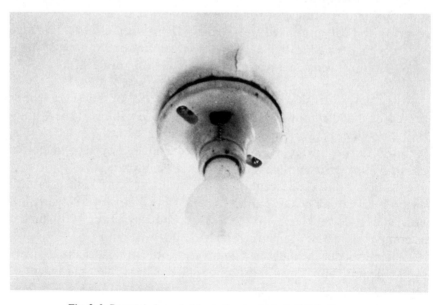

Fig. 2–3. Porcelain lamp holder is the simplest of all light fixtures.

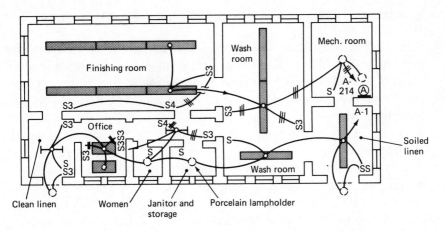

Fig. 2-4. Floor plan of lamp holder used in a janitor's closet.

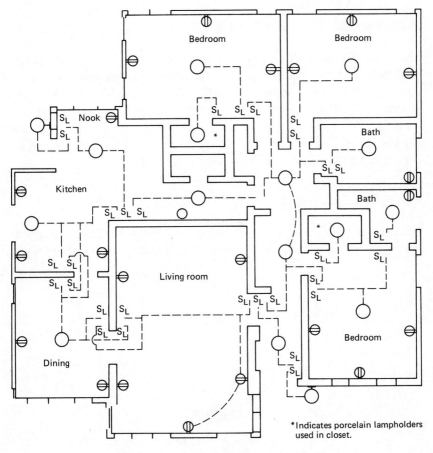

*Indicates porcelain lampholders used in closet.

Fig. 2-5. Porcelain lamp holder used in closet.

Since the lamp has no diffuser, it is not recommended for any lengthy seeing task because the glare puts too much strain on the eyes. It should also not be used in areas where the lamp could become damaged since there is no protection provided with this type of lighting fixture.

Porcelain lamp holders may also be used in clothes closets of homes on the wall above the closet door, provided the clearance between the fixture and a storage area where combustible material may be stored within the closet is not less than 18 inches, or on the ceiling over an area which is unobstructed to the floor, maintaining an 18-inch clearance horizontally between the fixture and a storage area where combustible material may be stored within the closet (Figure 2-5).

PENDANT DIFFUSING SPHERE

The pendant diffusing sphere in Figure 2-6 is typical of several available spheres. A candlepower distribution curve for this type of fixture is shown in Figure 2-7 while a coefficient of utilization table is shown in Figure 2-8. Note that the spacing-to-mounting-height ratio is 1.5; this means that this fixture may be spaced on 15-foot centers for a 10-foot mounting height above the work plane and still maintain a satisfactory uniformity of illumination.

Residential Applications

The pendant diffusing sphere is much used in residential applications, especially when a modern decor is used. As well as over bars, room

Fig. 2-6. Typical pendant diffusing sphere.

SPACING RATIO - 1.1

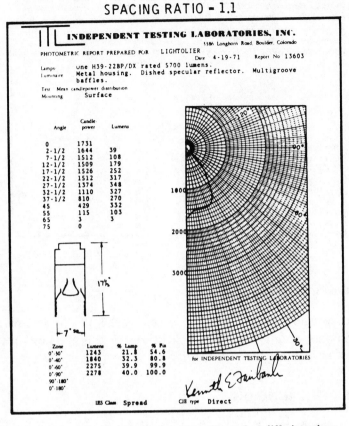

INDEPENDENT TESTING LABORATORIES, INC.
3386 Longhorn Road, Boulder, Colorado

PHOTOMETRIC REPORT PREPARED FOR   LIGHTOLIER
Date 4-19-71   Report No 13603

Lamps   une H39-22BP/DX rated 5700 lumens.
Luminaire   Metal housing. Dished specular reflector. Multigroove
               baffles.

Test   Mean candlepower distribution
Mounting   Surface

Angle	Candle-power	Lumens
0	1731	
2-1/2	1644	39
7-1/2	1512	108
12-1/2	1509	179
17-1/2	1526	252
22-1/2	1512	317
27-1/2	1374	348
32-1/2	1110	327
37-1/2	810	270
45	429	332
55	115	103
65	3	3
75	0	

Zone	Lumens	% Lamp	% Fix
0°-30°	1243	21.8	54.6
0°-40°	1840	32.3	80.8
0°-60°	2275	39.9	99.9
0°-90°	2278	40.0	100.0
90°-180°			
0°-180°			

IES Class Spread   CIE type Direct

for INDEPENDENT TESTING LABORATORIES

Fig. 2-7. Candlepower distribution curve of a pendant diffusing sphere.

dividers, and so forth, corridors and vestibules are good locations in which to use this fixture. Make sure the ceiling height is high enough before using this type of fixture—especially in a heavily traveled area.

Commercial Applications

Typical applications of pendant diffusing spheres include general/decorative lighting over information booths, lobby desks, restaurant booths and similar areas.

I.T.L. Report No. 13603C. These coefficients were computed by the Zonal-Cavity Method, I.E.S. Recommended Practice, and prepared from the candlepower distribution data given in Independent Testing Laboratories Report No. 13603, dated 4/19/71, and are based on a 20% Floor Cavity Reflectances.

	Ceiling Cavity Reflectance															
	80			70			50			30			10			0
Room Cavity Ratio	Wall Reflectance															
	50	30	10	50	30	10	50	30	10	50	30	10	50	30	10	0
	Coefficients of Utilization															
1	44	43	42	43	42	41	42	41	40	40	40	39	39	38	38	37
2	41	39	38	40	39	37	39	38	36	38	37	36	37	36	35	34
3	38	36	34	37	35	34	36	35	33	35	34	33	34	33	32	32
4	35	33	31	34	32	31	34	32	30	33	31	30	32	31	29	29
5	32	30	28	32	29	28	31	29	27	30	29	27	30	28	27	26
6	30	27	25	30	27	25	29	27	25	28	26	25	28	26	25	24
7	28	25	23	27	25	23	27	25	23	26	24	23	26	24	23	22
8	25	23	21	25	23	21	25	22	21	24	22	21	24	22	21	20
9	23	21	19	23	20	19	23	20	19	22	20	19	22	20	18	18
10	21	19	17	21	19	17	21	18	17	20	18	17	20	18	17	16

Fig. 2–8. Coefficient utilization table of pendant diffusion sphere.

Industrial Appplications

Decorative and general lighting in industrial reception areas and cafeterias are about the only applications of this type of fixture in industry and institutions.

CONCENTRIC RING UNIT

This type of fixture has long been used as a glare-free light source in such areas as school classrooms, offices, spectator areas of sports arenas, and the like. In nearly every application, silver-bowl incandescent lamps are used so that approximately 83% of the lamp lumens are directed upward to be reflected off the room ceiling. Figure 2–9 shows a typical concentric ring lighting fixture.

PORCELAIN-ENAMELED VENTILATED DOME

The porcelain-enameled ventilated dome (Figure 2–10) has always been a popular source of incandescent light in warehouses, store rooms, and work areas where appearance was secondary. This type of fixture is still being used quite extensively in warehouses that require

Typical Luminaire	Typical Distribution and Per Cent Lamp Lumens		ρ_{CC}[a] →	80			70			50			30			10			0	WDRC[e] →
	Maint. Cat.	Maximum S/MH Guide[d]	ρ_W[b] →	50	30	10	50	30	10	50	30	10	50	30	10	50	30	10	0	
			RCR[c] →	Coefficients of Utilization for 20 Per Cent Effective Floor Cavity Reflectance (ρ_{FC} = 20)																	
	II	1.5	0	.83	.83	.83	.71	.71	.71	.49	.49	.49	.30	.30	.30	.12	.12	.12	.03	.02
			1	.72	.69	.66	.62	.60	.57	.43	.42	.40	.26	.25	.25	.10	.10	.10	.03	.01
	83%↑		2	.63	.58	.54	.54	.50	.47	.38	.36	.33	.23	.22	.21	.09	.09	.08	.02	.01
	3½%↓		3	.55	.49	.45	.48	.43	.39	.33	.30	.28	.20	.19	.17	.08	.08	.07	.02	.01
			4	.48	.42	.37	.42	.37	.33	.29	.26	.24	.18	.16	.15	.07	.07	.06	.02	.01
			5	.43	.36	.32	.37	.32	.28	.26	.23	.20	.16	.14	.13	.06	.06	.05	.01	.01
			6	.38	.32	.27	.33	.28	.24	.23	.20	.17	.14	.12	.11	.06	.05	.04	.01	.01
Concentric ring unit with incandescent silvered-bowl lamp			7	.34	.28	.23	.30	.24	.21	.21	.17	.15	.13	.11	.09	.05	.04	.04	.01	.01
			8	.31	.25	.20	.27	.21	.18	.19	.15	.13	.12	.10	.08	.05	.04	.03	.01	.01
			9	.28	.22	.18	.24	.19	.16	.17	.14	.11	.10	.09	.07	.04	.03	.03	.01	.01
			10	.25	.20	.16	.22	.17	.14	.16	.12	.10	.10	.08	.06	.04	.03	.03	.01	.01

Fig. 2–9. Typical concentric ring lighting fixture.

41

STANDARD DOME

Fig. 2-10. Porcelain-enameled ventilated dome.

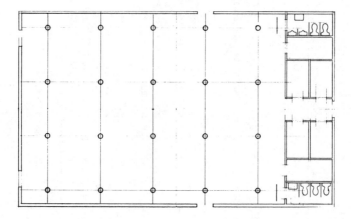

Fig. 2-11. Floor plan showing the application of ventilated dome fixtures.

illumination only at infrequent intervals. In areas where prolonged illumination is required, incandescent lighting fixtures are being replaced with fluorescent or HID lighting to conserve energy. Because of its low installation cost, a very practical modern-day use for this fixture would be in janitors' closets and storage closets of all commercial, institutional and industrial types. A floor plan showing the use of this fixture is shown in Figure 2-11.

PRISMATIC SQUARE SURFACE DRUM

The prismatic square surface drum is another type of incandescent lighting fixture that is used in janitors' and storage closets and other areas where light is used only periodically, and where a more pleasing appearance is required than can be achieved with dome lights.

At one time, this type of fixture was used quite extensively in corridors of commercial and institutional buildings. However, due to the recent focus on energy conservation, most such lights have been replaced with fluorescent fixtures (Figure 2–12).

RECESSED FIXTURE WITHOUT SHIELDING

A recessed fixture without shielding is very popular for use as accent lighting in both residences and commerce. An R–40 floodlamp is almost always the lamp source used.

RECESSED FIXTURE WITH
SPECULAR ANODIZED REFLECTOR

A fixture similar to the one just described, except that most have a 45° cutoff that hides the lamp source from viewers better than does the recessed fixture without shielding. Recessed fixtures with specular anodized reflectors are used for all types of commercial applications, especially in stores where true color rendition and details of the product are important (Figure 2–13).

RECESSED FIXTURE WITH
2-INCH DIAMETER APERTURE

A type of fixture used almost exclusively for accent lighting on an object or person. Figure 2–14 shows the physical and utilization characteristics of recessed fixtures with 2-inch diameter apertures, and Figure 2–15 shows an application of these fixtures to highlight the speaker in a men's Sunday School classroom.

REFLECTOR DOWNLIGHT WITH BAFFLES

An excellent light source for supplementary lighting in commercial applications. The built-in baffles help to prevent direct glare and shadows (Figure 2–16). The main purpose of the baffles is to shield

Typical Luminaire	Typical Distribution and Per Cent Lamp Lumens		$\rho_{CC}{}^a \rightarrow$	80			70			50			30			10			0	
	Maint. Cat.	Maximum S/MH Guide[d]	$\rho_W{}^b \rightarrow$	50	30	10	50	30	10	50	30	10	50	30	10	50	30	10	0	WDRC[e] $\rightarrow$
	V	1.3	RCR[c] $\rightarrow$	Coefficients of Utilization for 20 Per Cent Effective Floor Cavity Reflectance ($\rho_{FC} = 20$)																
	18½% ↑		0	.89	.89	.89	.85	.85	.85	.77	.77	.77	.70	.70	.70	.63	.63	.63	.60	.24
	60½% ↓		1	.78	.75	.72	.74	.72	.69	.68	.66	.64	.62	.60	.58	.56	.55	.54	.51	.20
			2	.69	.65	.61	.66	.62	.58	.61	.57	.54	.56	.53	.50	.51	.49	.47	.44	.18
			3	.62	.57	.52	.60	.55	.50	.55	.51	.47	.50	.47	.44	.46	.44	.41	.39	.16
			4	.56	.50	.46	.54	.49	.44	.50	.45	.42	.46	.42	.39	.42	.39	.37	.35	.15
Prismatic square surface drum			5	.51	.45	.40	.49	.43	.39	.45	.41	.37	.42	.38	.35	.39	.36	.33	.31	.13
			6	.46	.40	.36	.45	.39	.35	.42	.37	.33	.39	.35	.31	.36	.32	.30	.28	.13
			7	.42	.36	.32	.41	.35	.31	.38	.33	.29	.35	.31	.28	.33	.29	.27	.25	.12
			8	.39	.32	.28	.37	.32	.28	.35	.30	.26	.32	.28	.25	.30	.27	.24	.22	.12
			9	.35	.29	.25	.34	.29	.25	.32	.27	.24	.30	.26	.23	.28	.24	.22	.20	.11
			10	.32	.27	.23	.31	.26	.22	.29	.25	.21	.27	.23	.20	.26	.22	.20	.18	.11

Fig. 2–12. Prismatic square surface drum.

44

Fig. 2-13

IV 0.7

0% ↑
85% ↓

R-40 flood with specular anodized reflector skirt; 45° cutoff

0	1.00	1.00	1.00	.98	.98	.98	.94	.94	.94	.90	.90	.90	.86	.86	.86	.84	.08
1	.96	.94	.92	.94	.92	.91	.90	.89	.88	.87	.86	.85	.84	.84	.83	.82	.08
2	.91	.88	.86	.90	.87	.85	.87	.85	.83	.84	.83	.82	.82	.81	.80	.79	.08
3	.87	.84	.81	.86	.83	.81	.84	.81	.79	.82	.80	.78	.80	.78	.77	.76	.07
4	.83	.80	.77	.82	.79	.77	.81	.78	.76	.79	.77	.75	.78	.76	.74	.73	.07
5	.79	.76	.73	.79	.75	.72	.77	.74	.72	.76	.73	.71	.75	.73	.71	.70	.07
6	.76	.73	.70	.76	.72	.70	.75	.72	.69	.74	.71	.69	.73	.70	.68	.67	.07
7	.73	.69	.66	.73	.70	.66	.72	.68	.66	.71	.68	.66	.70	.67	.65	.64	.07
8	.70	.66	.63	.70	.66	.63	.69	.65	.63	.68	.65	.63	.67	.65	.63	.62	.07
9	.67	.63	.60	.67	.63	.60	.66	.62	.60	.65	.62	.60	.65	.62	.60	.59	.07
10	.64	.60	.58	.64	.60	.58	.63	.60	.58	.63	.60	.57	.62	.59	.57	.56	.07

Fig. 2-13. Recessed fixture with specular anodized reflector.

Fig. 2-14

IV 0.7

0% ↑
43½% ↓

EAR-38 lamp above 2" diameter aperture

0	.51	.51	.51	.50	.50	.50	.48	.48	.48	.46	.46	.46	.44	.44	.44	.43	.04
1	.49	.48	.48	.48	.48	.47	.47	.46	.46	.45	.45	.44	.44	.43	.43	.42	.03
2	.47	.46	.45	.46	.45	.44	.45	.44	.43	.43	.43	.42	.43	.42	.42	.41	.03
3	.45	.44	.43	.45	.43	.42	.44	.42	.42	.43	.42	.41	.42	.41	.40	.40	.03
4	.43	.42	.41	.43	.41	.40	.42	.41	.40	.41	.40	.39	.41	.40	.39	.38	.03
5	.42	.40	.39	.41	.40	.38	.41	.39	.38	.40	.39	.38	.39	.38	.38	.37	.03
6	.40	.39	.37	.40	.38	.37	.39	.38	.37	.39	.38	.37	.38	.37	.36	.36	.03
7	.39	.37	.36	.39	.37	.36	.38	.37	.35	.38	.36	.35	.37	.36	.35	.35	.03
8	.37	.36	.34	.37	.35	.34	.37	.35	.33	.36	.35	.34	.36	.35	.34	.33	.03
9	.36	.34	.33	.36	.34	.33	.35	.34	.33	.35	.34	.33	.35	.34	.33	.32	.03
10	.35	.33	.32	.35	.33	.32	.34	.33	.32	.34	.33	.32	.34	.32	.31	.31	.03

Fig. 2-14. Physical and utilization characteristics of a recessed fixture with 2-inch diameter aperture.

Fig. 2-15. Practical application of the fixture in Figure 2-14.

the light source from direct view at certain angles, or to absorb un-wanted light.

Typical uses include mounting directly over desks or work counters to supplement the lighting over the work areas. For example, a room may be lit with recessed fluorescent fixtures for general illumination with a few reflector downlights with baffles mounted directly over a secretary's typing area or work area.

MEDIUM DISTRIBUTION UNIT WITH LENS PLATE

This type of lighting fixture (Figure 2-17) is used for general illumi-nation in recreation rooms in homes, for supplementary lighting in commerce, or for inspection in industry where high visibility with comfort is required. For example, newspaper proofreading, detecting punch or scribe marks on dull metal, detecting wax marks on auto bodies, and other jobs where it is necessary to create bright reflection from detail are applications for the medium distribution unit with lens plate.

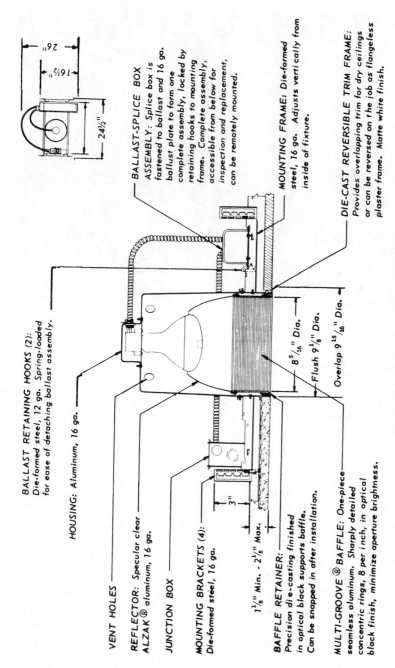

BALLAST RETAINING HOOKS (2):
Die-formed steel, 12 ga. Spring-loaded
for ease of detaching ballast assembly.

HOUSING: Aluminum, 16 ga.

VENT HOLES

REFLECTOR: Specular clear
ALZAK® aluminum, 16 ga.

JUNCTION BOX

MOUNTING BRACKETS (4):
Die-formed steel, 16 ga.

BAFFLE RETAINER:
Precision di e-casting finished
in optical black supports baffle.
Can be snapped in after installation.

MULTI-GROOVE ® BAFFLE: One-piece
seamless aluminum. Sharply detailed
concentric rings, 8 per inch, in optical
black finish, minimize aperture brightness.

BALLAST-SPLICE BOX
ASSEMBLY: Splice box is
fastened to ballast and 16 ga.
ballast plate to form one
complete assembly, locked by
retaining hooks to mounting
frame. Complete assembly,
accessible from below for
inspection and replacement,
can be remotely mounted.

MOUNTING FRAME: Die-formed
steel, 16 ga. Adjusts verti cally from
inside of fixture.

DIE-CAST REVERSIBLE TRIM FRAME:
Provides overlapping trim for dry ceilings
or can be reversed on the job as flangeless
plaster frame. Matte white finish.

$8\frac{5}{16}$" Dia.

Flush $9\frac{1}{8}$" Dia.

Overlap $9\frac{15}{16}$" Dia.

$1\frac{1}{8}$" Min. - $2\frac{1}{8}$" Max.

3"

26"

$16\frac{1}{2}$"

$24\frac{1}{2}$"

Fig. 2–16. Reflector downlight with baffles.

Fig. 2-17. Medium distribution unit with lens plate.

WIDE DISTRIBUTION UNIT WITH LENS PLATE

This type of lighting fixture (Figure 2-18) is used extensively in residences for general illumination (almost always used in multiple) in recreation rooms, kitchens, laundries, halls, and so forth. The wide distribution unit is used singly or in small groups for small areas such as walk-in closets, garages, entry doors, overhangs in porches, and the like.

Because of high energy consumption (as compared with other types of light sources), this type of fixture is seldom used in commerce or industry for general illumination, with the exception of areas where an incandescent light source is necessary to provide proper color rendition. For example, the floor plan in Figure 2-19 shows wide distribution incandescent units used in a church basement social hall where weekly dinners are served. The recessed incandescent lighting fixtures were chosen, because of the low ceiling height, to compliment people's complexions and to provide a more pleasing color rendition to the food than would have other light sources.

Fig. 2-18. Wide distribution unit with lens plate.

Typical Luminaire	Typical Distribution and Per Cent Lamp Lumens		ρ_{CC} →	80			70			50			30			10			0	WDRC[e] →
	Maint. Cat.	Maximum S/MH Guide[d]	ρ_W[b] →	50	30	10	50	30	10	50	30	10	50	30	10	50	30	10	0	0
			RCR[c] →	Coefficients of Utilization for 20 Per Cent Effective Floor Cavity Reflectance (ρ_{FC} = 20)																
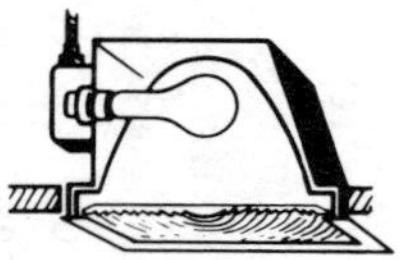	V 1.4		0	.63	.63	.63	.62	.62	.62	.59	.59	.59	.56	.56	.56	.54	.54	.54	.53	.14
		0%	1	.58	.56	.54	.57	.55	.54	.54	.53	.52	.52	.51	.50	.50	.50	.49	.48	.13
		53½%	2	.53	.50	.48	.52	.49	.47	.50	.48	.46	.48	.47	.45	.47	.45	.44	.43	.12
			3	.48	.45	.42	.47	.44	.42	.46	.43	.41	.44	.42	.40	.43	.41	.40	.39	.12
			4	.44	.40	.37	.43	.40	.37	.42	.39	.37	.41	.38	.36	.40	.38	.36	.35	.12
			5	.40	.36	.33	.39	.36	.33	.38	.35	.33	.37	.35	.32	.36	.34	.32	.31	.11
			6	.36	.32	.30	.36	.32	.29	.35	.32	.29	.34	.31	.29	.33	.31	.29	.28	.11
			7	.33	.29	.26	.33	.29	.26	.32	.28	.26	.31	.28	.26	.30	.28	.26	.25	.10
			8	.30	.26	.23	.30	.26	.23	.29	.26	.23	.28	.25	.23	.28	.25	.23	.22	.10
			9	.27	.23	.21	.27	.23	.21	.26	.23	.21	.26	.23	.20	.25	.22	.20	.19	.09
			10	.25	.21	.18	.25	.21	.18	.24	.21	.18	.24	.20	.18	.23	.20	.18	.17	.09

Wide distribution unit with lens plate and inside frost lamp

49

Fig. 2-19. Wide distribution incandescent units used in a church basement social hall.

RECESSED FIXTURE WITH DROPPED DIFFUSING GLASS

There are many variations of this fixture type, but most are usually characterized by an opaque or partly opaque side or border as shown in Figure 2-20. This restricts the distribution somewhat and limits the effectiveness as a general lighting source.

Such fixtures are still used in vestibules and corridors of churches and in homes or apartment buildings. Some other typical applications are shown in Figure 2-21.

ENCLOSED REFLECTOR

This type of fixture (Figure 2-22) is used mainly in industry for supplementary lighting on assembly lines or inspection areas where an incandescent light source is necessary for the visual task. Such areas would include emphasizing surface breaks on opaque materials, producing visibility of details within material such as bubbles as well as surface details such as scratches on transparent materials, emphasizing detail with a poor contrast, or emphasizing surface irregularities.

	Typical Distribution and Per Cent Lamp Lumens		Maximum S/MH Guide[d]	ρ_{CC} [a] →	80			70			50			30			10			0	WDRC[e] →
Typical Luminaire	Maint. Cat.			ρ_W [b] →	50	30	10	50	30	10	50	30	10	50	30	10	50	30	10	0	
	V	1.3		RCR[c] →	Coefficients of Utilization for 20 Per Cent Effective Floor Cavity Reflectance ($\rho_{FC} = 20$)																
				0	.61	.61	.61	.60	.60	.60	.57	.57	.57	.54	.54	.54	.51	.51	.51	.50	
				1	.53	.51	.48	.52	.50	.47	.49	.47	.46	.47	.45	.44	.45	.44	.42	.41	.23
				2	.46	.42	.39	.45	.42	.39	.43	.40	.38	.41	.39	.37	.39	.37	.35	.34	.20
				3	.40	.36	.33	.40	.35	.32	.38	.34	.31	.36	.33	.31	.35	.32	.30	.29	.18
				4	.36	.31	.28	.35	.31	.28	.34	.30	.27	.33	.29	.26	.31	.28	.26	.25	.16
				5	.32	.27	.24	.31	.27	.24	.30	.26	.23	.29	.25	.23	.28	.25	.22	.21	.15
				6	.29	.24	.20	.28	.24	.20	.27	.23	.20	.26	.22	.20	.25	.22	.19	.18	.13
				7	.26	.21	.18	.25	.21	.18	.24	.20	.17	.23	.20	.17	.22	.19	.17	.16	.12
				8	.23	.19	.16	.23	.18	.15	.22	.18	.15	.21	.18	.15	.20	.17	.15	.14	.11
				9	.21	.17	.14	.21	.16	.14	.20	.16	.13	.19	.16	.13	.19	.15	.13	.12	.11
				10	.19	.15	.12	.19	.15	.12	.18	.14	.12	.18	.14	.12	.17	.14	.12	.11	.10

Recessed unit with dropped diffusing glass

$1\frac{1}{2}\%$

$50\frac{1}{2}\%$

Fig. 2-20. Recessed fixture with dropped diffusing glass.

Fig. 2-21. Typical applications of the fixture in Figure 20.

OPERATING CHARACTERISTICS

Both the life of a lamp and its light output are determined by its filament temperature. The higher the temperature for a given lamp, the greater the efficacy (lumens emitted per watt of power consumed) and the shorter the life. Hence light output and life are interdependent. A lamp can be designed for a long life at the expense of light output, or for high light output at the expense of life. In practice, the life for which a lamp is designed is an economic balance between the two factors, determined on the basis of the purpose for which the lamp is to be used.

Obviously, the quality or value of a lamp cannot be judged by its life alone. Lamp life may be as short as 10-50 hours for projection lamps and 3 hours for photoflood lamps, where high light output is the dominant requirement, replacement is convenient, and life is of relatively little consequence. Or it may be as long as 2000-6000 hours for street lighting lamps, where the high cost of replacing burned out lamps justifies relatively low efficacies. For general lighting service

Typical Luminaire	Typical Distribution and Per Cent Lamp Lumens		ρ_{CC} →	80			70			50			30			10			0	WDRC[e] →
	Maint. Cat.	Maximum S/MH Guide[d]	ρ_W[b] →	50	30	10	50	30	10	50	30	10	50	30	10	50	30	10	0	
			RCR[c] →	Coefficients of Utilization for 20 Per Cent Effective Floor Cavity Reflectance (ρ_{FC} = 20)																
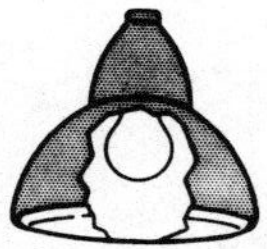	V	1.4	0	.85	.85	.85	.83	.83	.83	.79	.79	.79	.76	.76	.76	.73	.73	.73	.71	
	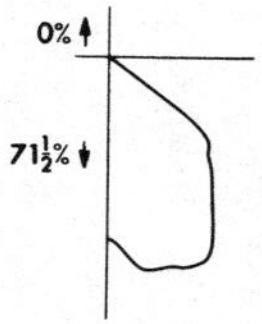		1	.78	.76	.74	.76	.74	.73	.73	.72	.70	.71	.69	.68	.68	.67	.66	.65	.17
			2	.71	.68	.65	.70	.67	.64	.68	.65	.63	.65	.63	.61	.63	.62	.60	.59	.16
			3	.65	.61	.57	.64	.60	.57	.62	.59	.56	.60	.57	.55	.59	.56	.54	.53	.16
			4	.60	.55	.51	.59	.54	.51	.57	.53	.50	.55	.52	.50	.54	.51	.49	.48	.15
			5	.54	.49	.45	.54	.49	.45	.52	.48	.45	.51	.47	.44	.50	.46	.44	.43	.14
			6	.49	.44	.40	.49	.44	.40	.47	.43	.40	.46	.42	.40	.45	.42	.39	.38	.14
			7	.44	.39	.35	.44	.39	.35	.43	.38	.35	.42	.38	.35	.41	.37	.35	.33	.14
			8	.40	.35	.31	.40	.35	.31	.39	.35	.31	.38	.34	.31	.38	.34	.31	.30	.13
			9	.37	.31	.28	.36	.31	.28	.36	.31	.28	.35	.31	.28	.34	.30	.27	.26	.13
			10	.33	.28	.25	.33	.28	.25	.32	.28	.25	.32	.28	.25	.31	.27	.24	.23	.12

Enclosed reflector with an in-candescent lamp

0%

71½%

Fig. 2–22. Enclosed reflector.

lamps, where long life is desirable but replacement is comparatively easy, a life of 750 or 1000 hours has become the accepted standard.

Published data on lamp life refer to the average life of a group of lamps under specified test conditions, and are not intended as a guarantee of the performance of any individual lamp. As shown by the accompanying mortality curve, in any large group of lamps some will fail relatively early in life, whereas others will still be burning long after the end of rated life (Figure 2–23).

As a general rule, lamps should be burned at rated voltage. Over-voltage operation results in higher wattage, higher efficacy, and higher light output—but shorter lamp life. Undervoltage burning, while increasing lamp life, causes a reduction in wattage, in efficacy, and in light output. A voltage of as little as 5% below normal results in a loss of light amounting to more than 16%, with a saving in wattage of only 8%. Since lamp cost is almost always small compared with the cost of the power to operate the lamp, the increased lamp life which accompanies reduced voltage does not begin to compensate economically for the loss in light output. Maintenance of the proper voltage is therefore an important factor in obtaining good performance from lamps and lighting installations.

However, there are cases where it is more economical to operate lamps at higher than rated voltage. The cost of power, the cost of fixtures and wiring, the cost of lamps, and the increased light output, must be taken into consideration in estimating the possible advantages of overvoltage operation. The power cost must be computed on the basis of the increased wattage at the higher voltage, and the figure for lamp cost must take into account the shortened life as well as the

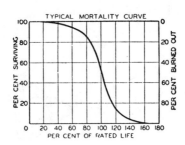

Fig. 2–23. Typical mortality curve for incandescent lamps.

cost of lamp replacement. In some cases, the higher light output may make possible a reduction in the number of lighting units required.

Where the hours of burning for a season or period are relatively short and the energy cost is comparatively high, and particularly where the lamps are replaced in a group before burnout, careful analysis may reveal a definite saving in operating the lamps at over-voltage. These conditions are often encountered in certain types of sports lighting, where overvoltage lamp operation is a rather common practice, as for example the use of 110–volt lamps on a 120–volt circuit.

Any calculation of lamp and energy costs emphasizes the fact that the cost of lamps is nearly always a minor consideration compared to the cost of power. Under ordinary circumstances, the lamps represent less than 10% of the cost of lamps and energy combined. Thus, the efficacy of a lamp is more important than its price, and low-efficacy sources should not be used except in special cases where long life is a prime requisite. It is more economical to discard lamps that have been in service a long time and are seriously blackened than to continue to operate them to burnout at their depreciated efficacy. In many cases it is desirable to replace all the lamps in an installation at the same time, before the majority of them have reached the end of their useful life. This practice is commonly called group replacement or group relamping.

Because an incandescent lamp burns at constant voltage, the filament gradually evaporates or sublimes, causing a slow but continuous reduction in wattage and light output. The normal end of life is reached when the wire breaks or burns through at its thinnest spot. A further reduction in light output results from the absorption of light by the vaporized tungsten, which collects as a black deposit on the inner surface of the bulb. Some projection and bipost base general-service lamps are provided with a screen or grid located above the filament to collect the blackening as it is carried upward by the gas currents within the bulb and to prevent it from being deposited on the bulb walls. The use of a collector screen materially improves the lumen maintenance of a lamp, and makes it possible to employ a smaller bulb than would otherwise be feasible. Some high-wattage high-efficacy lamps are made with a small amount of loose tungsten

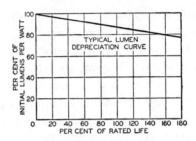

Fig. 2-24. Typical lumen depreciation curve for incandescent lamps.

powder in the bulb that can be agitated to clean the blackening from the inner surface of the glass by a scouring action.

The rate of lumen depreciation varies considerably among different types of lamps. Approximate mean lumens for most of the commonly used higher wattage general lighting service lamps are included in Figure 2-24. The approximate mean lumens (average light output throughout life) is especially significant in estimating the maintenance factor of a lighting installation.

TYPES OF INCANDESCENT LAMPS

General Lighting Service Lamps

The familiar general lighting service lamps, from the 15-watt A–15 to the 1500-watt PS–52, designed for multiple burning on 120-, 125-, or 130-volt circuits, are the most commonly used filament-type lamps. All standard general service lamps are equipped with screw bases. The larger wattages are manufactured in either clear or inside-frosted bulbs. Below 150 watts, inside-frosted and inside white silica coated lamps are standard. The wattages most commonly used in the home are available in a straight-sided modified T-bulb shape, with the white silica coating.

High-and Low-Voltage Lamps

Lamps similar to those of the standard-voltage line are available for operation on 230 and 250 volts. The low efficacy of these lamps, as compared to similar lamps of standard-voltage rating, has already

been mentioned. Other disadvantages resulting from the smaller filament wire diameter of high-voltage lamps are reduced mechanical
strength, and larger overall light-source size which makes them less
satisfactory for use in floodlight and projection equipment. The only
gain achieved by the industrial use of thse higher voltages is the reduction in ampere load which results from doubling the voltage, and
the consequent saving in wiring cost. Lamps for operation on 30-
and 60-volt circuits are also available for use in train lighting and in
rural home service.

Projector and Reflector Lamps

Par-built (projector) and R-bulb (reflector) lamps combine in one
unit a light source and a highly efficient sealed-in reflector consisting
of vaporized aluminum or silver applied to the inner surface of the
bulb. The 100-watt PAR-38 and 150-watt R-40 lamps are available
in several colors. PAR bulbs are made of hard glass. PAR lamps up to
150 watts in size, as well as a few special service R lamps with heat-
resistant-glass bulbs, can be used outdoors without danger of breakage
from rain or snow. Larger PAR lamps and all other R lamps are not
recommended for outdoor use unless protected from the elements.

Higher-wattage R-52 and R-57 reflector lamps are designed for
general lighting purposes. They are made in both wide and narrow
distributions, and are best adapted for high-ceilinged industrial
areas where the atmosphere contains noncombustible dirt, smoke, or
fumes. Where heat-resistant glass is required for protection against
thermal shock, the R-60 lamps will perform similarly to R-52 and
R-57 lamps. These latter types are especially suited for outdoor
floodlighting.

Showcase and Lumiline Lamps

Low-wattage tubular-bulb lamps are used for showcase lighting and
other applications where small bulb diameter is required. Some of
these are designed to be used in reflectors, and others are provided
with an internal reflecting surface extending over approximately half
the bulb area, which concentrates the light to form a beam. The

FILAMENT LAMPS

REPRESENTATIVE STANDARD-VOLTAGE FILAMENT LAMPS

GENERAL LIGHTING SERVICE

Watts	Bulb	Finish	Base	Max. Over-all Length (Inches)	Fila-ment	Rated Avg. Life (Hrs.)	Approx. Initial Lumens	Approx. Mean Lumens
25	A-19	I.F.	Medium	3 15/16	C-9	1600	240	....
40	T-19	White	Medium	4 7/16	C-9	1750	425	....
60	T-19	White	Medium	4 7/16	CC-8	1350	840	....
75	T-19	White	Medium	4 7/16	CC-8	1150	1110	....
100	T-19	White	Medium	4 7/16	CC-8	1000	1600	....
50							610	....
100	T-19	White	3-Contact Medium	5 5/16	2CC-6	1600	1460	....
150							2070	....
100							1500	....
200	PS-25	White	3-Contact Mogul	6 13/16	2CC-6	1200	3400	....
300							4900	....
150	T-21	White	Medium	5 1/2	CC-8	1000	2550	....
200	A-23	I.F., Cl.	Medium	6 5/16	CC-8	750	3900	3600
300	PS-25		Medium	6 15/16	CC-8	750	6300	5800
500	PS-35	I.F.	Mogul	9 3/8	CC-8	1000	10750	10000
750	PS-52	or	Mogul	13 1/16	2CC-8	1000	16700	15500
1000	PS-52	Clear	Mogul	13 1/16	2CC-8	1000	23000	21000
1500	PS-52		Mogul	13 1/16	C-7A	1000	33300	27000

PROJECTOR AND REFLECTOR SERVICE
(2000-Hour-Life Lamps)

Watts	Bulb	Base	Max. Over-all Length (Inches)	① Approx. Beam Spread (De-grees)	① Approx. Initial Beam Lumens	Approx. Initial Total Lumens	② Approx. Initial Max. Candle-power	Distri-bution
③Projector								
75	PAR-38	Med. Skt.	5 5/16	30	465	750	4800	Spot
75	PAR-38	Med. Skt.	5 5/16	60	600	750	1500	Flood
150	PAR-38	Med. Skt.	5 5/16	30	1100	1730	10500	Spot
150	PAR-38	Med. Skt.	5 5/16	60	1350	1730	3400	Flood
150	PAR-38	Med. Skt.	5 5/16	120	....	1730	1200	W. Flood
200	PAR-46	Med. Side	4	17 x 23	1200	2350	33000	Narrow
200	PAR-46	Prong	4	20 x 40	1300	2350	12000	Medium
300	PAR-56	Mogul	5	15 x 20	1800	3720	70000	Narrow
300	PAR-56	End	5	20 x 35	2000	3720	22000	Medium
300	PAR-56	Prong	5	30 x 60	2100	3720	10000	Wide
500	PAR-64	Extended	6	13 x 20	3250	6500	120000	Narrow
500	PAR-64	Mogul	6	20 x 35	3700	6500	35000	Medium
500	PAR-64	End Prong	6	35 x 65	3800	6500	12000	Wide
Reflector								
30	R-20	Medium	3 15/16	90	160	210	245	Flood
50	R-20	Medium	3 15/16	90	325	420	430	Flood
75	R-30	Medium	5 3/16	50	410	820	1840	Spot
75	R-30	Medium	5 3/16	130	700	820	430	Flood
150	R-40	Medium	6 1/2	40	860	1890	7000	Spot
150	④R-40	Medium	6 1/2	110	1600	1890	1300	Flood
300	④R-40	Medium	6 1/2	35	1300	3700	13500	Spot
300	④R-40	Medium	6 1/2	115	2800	3700	2500	Flood
500	③R-40	Mogul	7 1/4	35	3100	6500	22000	Spot
500	③R-40	Mogul	7 1/4	115	5400	6500	4800	Flood
500	R-57	Mogul	12	70	....	7850	.....	Narrow
500	R-52	Mogul	11 3/4	120	....	7850	.....	Wide
750	R-57	Mogul	12	70	....	12700	.....	Narrow
750	R-52	Mogul	11 3/4	120	....	12700	.....	Wide
1000	R-57	Mogul	12	70	....	17500	.....	Narrow
750	③R-60	Mogul	10 3/8	40	....	11800	......	Flood
1000	③R-60	Mogul	10 3/8	60	....	16800	......	Flood

① To 10% of maximum candlepower.
② Average in 10° central cone (total spread) for all lamps except PAR spots and narrow-beam lamps. For PAR spots and narrow-beam lamps, average in 5° central cone.
③ Heat-resistant glass bulb.
④ Also available with heat-resistant glass bulb.

Fig. 2-25. Characteristics of typical filament lamps.

lumiline lamp is a special type of tubular light source that has a filament extending the length of the lamp and connected at each end to a disc base which requires a special type of lamp holder. Lumiline lamps are considerably less efficient than conventional general lighting service lamps, but are useful where a linear source is necessary.

Spotlight, Floodlight and Projection Lamps

The characteristics of all lamps designed for spotlight, floodlight, and projection applications are: compact filaments accurately positioned with respect to the base for light control, relatively short life for high efficacy and luminance, comparatively small bulbs and restricted burning position. Since spotlight lamps must produce narrower, more intense beams than do floodlight lamps, they usually have smaller filaments and shorter lives. In projection lamps, the light source is still more concentrated and life is further reduced, with accompanying increased efficacy.

The objective in designing projection lamps is to fill the aperture of the projection system with a light source of high luminance and maximum uniformity. This is accomplished by arranging the filament coils in a single or double vertical plane and by using a base which accurately locates the filament with respect to the optical system. The biplane (C-13D) filament, with coils arranged in two parallel rows so placed that the coils of one row fill in the spaces between those of the other, has much greater uniformity and higher average luminance than does the single-row monoplane (C-13) filament. Many projection lamps have such small bulbs and operate at such high temperatures that they cannot be burned without continuous forced ventilation, and some have designed lives as short as ten hours. Lamps for use in certain types of projectors have an opaque coating on the top of the bulb to prevent the emission of stray light.

Halogen Lamps

The halogen lamp is a new concept in incandescent lamps. It uses a quartz envelope, the basis for its many advantages which include: compactness, thermal shock resistance, high efficacy, and almost perfect maintained light throughout life. Iodine is used in the lamp to create a chemical cycle with the sublimated tungsten to keep the bulb clean. The halogen lamp is used for floodlights, aviation, photography, special effects, photocopy, and other applications where its special features are desirable.

Infrared Lamps

Infrared lamps are essentially the same as lamps designed for illumination purposes, the principal difference between them being that of filament temperature. Since the production of light is not an objective, infrared lamps are designed to operate at a very low temperature, resulting in a low light output (about 7–8 lumens per watt) and a consequent reduction in glare. Another advantage of low filament temperature is long life. Theoretically, on the basis of filament evaporation alone, the life of infrared lamps is many thousands of hours, but because of the possibility of failure from shock, vibration, and other causes, the rated life is given merely as "in excess of 5000 hours."

Infrared lamps used in the home and for therapeutic purposes are commonly the convenient self-contained 250–watt R–10 bulb type with internal reflector and red bulb. Those used in industrial processes are of three types: reflector lamps (125–, 250–, and 375–watt R–40) clear G–30 bulb lamps (125, 250, 375, and 500 watts), and the more recently developed small linear sources in the T–3 quartz bulb. The latter bulbs are available in a number of sizes, the effective heating length and the voltage rating increasing with the wattage. Gold-plated or specular aluminum reflectors are most effective for use with unreflectorized infrared lamps.

Chapter 3

Lighting with Fluorescent Lamps

The fluorescent lamp (Figure 3-1) is an electrical discharge source where a mercury arc generates ultraviolet energy which in turn activates the phosphor coatings to produce light. The lamp takes a variety of shapes, the dominant one being a smooth, long, tubular shape of various diameters and lengths. Due to their negative resistance, fluorescent lamps require a ballast to start and limit the current flow through them.

PREHEAT LAMPS

Preheat lamps have bipin bases as shown in Figure 3-2 and are manufactured in sizes from 4 to 100 watts and 6 to 60 inches long. Either manual or automatic starters are required to produce a separate cycle for cathode heating prior to operation as shown in the wiring diagram in Figure 3-3. Some preheat lamps may be operated on trigger start circuits with *rapid start* starting characteristics.

RAPID START LAMPS

Rapid start lamps include a family of lamps requiring a preheat cycle, but unlike preheat lamps, do not require a separate starter. The types

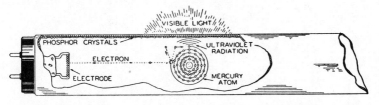

Fig. 3-1. Basic components of a fluorescent lamp.

of lamps falling under this classification are as follows:

1. *Rapid start bipin*—limited to 48 inches, 40–watt T–12 configuration. Operates at current of 430 M.A.
2. *High-output*—recessed double contact available in the range of 24 to 96 inches and from 35 to 110 watts, and operates at current of 800 M.A.
3. *Power groove*—recessed double contact lamp bases available in the range of 48 to 96 inches and from 110 to 215 watts in T–17 bulb size, and operates at current of 1500 M.A.
4. *VHO (very high output) and SHO (super high output)*—manufacturers' brand names for recessed double contact lamp bases in the range of 48 to 96 inches from 110 to 215 watts in T–12 bulb size, and operates at current of 1500 M.A.

Lamp operating characteristics are based upon their operation with ballasts. The data shown in Figure 3–4 are those established when operated with reference ballasts. Reference ballast design is established in conformance with A.S.A. Standard C82.3.

HOT CATHODE

Fig. 3–2. Preheat lamps have bipin bases.

TWO-LAMP PREHEAT CIRCUIT

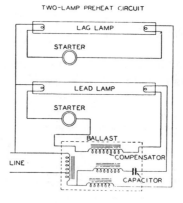

Fig. 3–3. Wiring diagram for a lighting fixture utilizing preheat lamps.

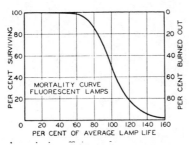

Fig. 3–4. Light operating characteristics.

Commercial ballast designs usually approach these performance ratings in various degrees depending upon the type of ballast used. Information regarding lamp performance with commercial ballast is available from the manufacturers—a sample of which is shown in Figure 3–5.

A further qualification of lamp performance, and specifically light output, is the lamp ambient temperature. Lamp ratings are based upon a lamp ambient of 79°F in still air. Temperatures below or above this rating point will result in lower light output, and account in part for luminaire efficiency where lamps are completely enclosed— resulting in increased lamp ambients above 79°F.

All fluorescent lamps produce radio frequency interference in varying amounts. This interference is radiated directly, or it is conducted and/or reradiated by means of the supply lines to the luminaire. The susceptibility of equipment to radiated interference will depend upon the distance from the lamp and the sensitivity of the equipment. A distance of 9 feet or more between equipment and lamp will negate the radiated interference. For conducted interference, a simple solution is the use of a line filter mounted within the fixture proper.

The following sections give design characteristics of fluorescent lighting fixtures and practical applications of each type described.

PORCELAIN-ENAMELED REFLECTOR
WITH 14° SHIELDING

This type of fluorescent lighting fixture (Figure 3–6) projects approximately 74% of the light downward and 13% of the light upward and

REFERENCE DATA—WESTINGHOUSE BALLASTS
FOR SLIMLINE AND RAPID START (425, 800, 1500 Ma.)

| Type Number | Lamp Data | | | Electrical Data | | | | | | Sound Rating | Min. Lamp Start Temp. °F① |
	Type	No. and Watts	Listing	Nominal Circuit Volts②	Approx. Line Current	Approx. Watts Loss	Approx. Input Watts	Open Circuit Volts	Recomm. GMF Fuse		
425 Ma, High Power Factor, Rapid Start											
C140R118LG	F40	1-40	CBM	118	.50	...	54	230	1.0	A	50
C140R277LG	F40	1-40	CBM	277	.21	...	54	230	0.5	A	50
U230R120LG	F30T12	2-30	UL	120	.65	...	76	250	1.6	A	50
U230R277LG	F30T12	2-30	UL	277	.28	...	76	250	0.8	A	50
C240R120LG	F40	2-40	CBM	120	.80	...	94	290	1.6	A	50
C240R240	F40	2-40	CBM	240	.41	...	94	290	0.8	A	50
C240R277LG	F40	2-40	CBM	277	.35	...	94	290	0.8	A	50
800 Ma, High Power Factor, Rapid Start											
C196H118LG	F96T12/HO	1-105	CBM	118	1.20	...	138	365	2.5	C	50
C196H277LG	F96T12/HO	1-105	CBM	277	.50	...	138	365	1.0	C	50
U248H118LG	F48T12/HO	2-60	UL	118	1.20	...	145	290	2.5	D	50
U248H277LG	F48T12/HO	2-60	UL	277	.53	...	147	290	1.0	D	50
C296H120LG	F96T12/HO	2-105	CBM	120	2.10	...	245	525	5.0	C	50
C296H277LG	F96T12/HO	2-105	CBM	277	.91	...	245	525	2.0	C	50
1500 Ma, SHO, High Power Factor, Rapid Start											
U248E118LG	F48T12/SHO	2-110	UL	118	2.10	...	240	295	4.0	E	0
U248E277LG	F48T12/SHO	2-110	UL	277	.92	...	240	295	2.0	E	0
U272E120LG	F72T12/SHO	2-106	UL	120	3.30	...	360	525	6.25	D	-20
U296E120	F96T12/SHO	2-215	UL	120	3.80	...	470	565	6.25	E	-20
C296E120LG	F96T12/SHO	2-215	CBM	120	3.60	...	460	525	6.25	D	0
U272E277LG	F72T12/SHO	2-160	UL	277	1.45	...	360	525	3.2	D	-20
C296E277LG	F96T12/SHO	2-215	CBM	277	1.70	...	460	525	3.2	D	0

Fig. 3–5. Sample of lamp performance data with commercial ballasts.

COEFFICIENTS OF UTILIZATION

LUMINAIRE	DISTRIBUTION	Spacing Not to Exceed	Reflectances										
			Ceiling Cavity	80%			50%			10%			0%
			Walls	50%	30%	10%	50%	30%	10%	50%	30%	10%	0%
Category III		1.3 x Mounting Height	RCR	Coefficients of Utilization									
Ventilated Dome Reflector			1	.85	.82	.79	.79	.77	.75	.73	.72	.71	.69
			2	.74	.69	.65	.70	.66	.62	.65	.62	.59	.58
			3	.65	.60	.54	.62	.57	.53	.57	.54	.51	.49
			4	.58	.51	.46	.55	.49	.45	.51	.47	.44	.42
			5	.50	.44	.38	.47	.42	.37	.45	.40	.36	.35
			6	.44	.38	.33	.43	.36	.32	.40	.35	.32	.30
			7	.40	.33	.28	.38	.33	.28	.36	.32	.27	.26
			8	.36	.29	.24	.34	.28	.24	.32	.27	.23	.22
			9	.33	.25	.20	.31	.25	.20	.29	.24	.20	.18
			10	.29	.22	.18	.28	.22	.18	.26	.21	.18	.17

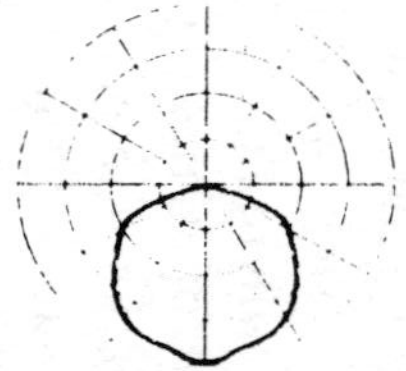

Fig. 3–6. Porcelain-enamel reflector with 14° shielding.

is known as a semidirect lighting source. The footcandles effective under this system at normal working planes are primarily a result of the light coming directly from the lighting fixture. The portion of the light directed to the ceiling results in a relatively small indirect component, the greatest value of which is that it brightens the ceiling area around the fixture and thus lowers the brightness contrasts.

In areas where appearance is unimportant, porcelain-enameled reflectors may be used for general lighting in storage areas of commercial buildings such as department stores. These are also good light sources for localized general lighting in commerce and industry; that is, the positioning of the fixtures with reference to particular work areas where high intensities are necessary. The "spill" light from these same lighting fixtures will then provide sufficient illumination for adjacent areas. Examples would be to light work points of large machines, sales counters in merchandising operations, and bench locations in factories or in home workshops.

Supplementary lighting is another use for the porcelain-enameled reflector when used in conjunction with general or localized general illumination. This sort of lighting fixture is frequently necessary where especially critical seeing tasks are involved, where it is not feasible to provide the desired intensity by either general or localized general lighting, and where light of a directional quality is required for certain inspection operations. Care must always be exercised to keep a reasonable relationship between the intensities of the general illumination and the supplementary lighting, since an excessive luminance ratio between the work point and its surroundings creates an uncomfortable seeing condition.

REFLECTOR WITH 35° SHIELDING

Another semidirect fluorescent lighting fixture that has the same applications as the fixture discussed in the previous paragraphs.

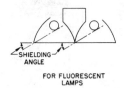

SHIELDING
ANGLE

FOR FLUORESCENT
LAMPS

Fig. 3–7. Reflector with 35° shielding.

However, the shielding angle is 35° on this fixture rather than 14° (Figure 3-7).

PORCELAIN-ENAMELED REFLECTOR WITH BAFFLES

A semidirect fluorescent luminaire that is suitable for general lighting in low bay areas of industrial applications since the baffles improve visual comfort.

In areas with a light-colored ceiling, luminance ratios between the ceiling and the luminaires are considerably lower when semidirect fixtures of this type are used than when totally direct fixtures are used. The upward light in this type of fixture usually comes from slots or holes in the top of the reflector. The openings not only transmit light, but also provide an outlet for the air currents created by the heat of the lamps. This ventilation cools the lamps, and the luminaire efficiency is raised because the lamps operate at a lower and more efficient temperature.

Both field and laboratory measurements show conclusively that ventilated lighting fixtures collect dirt much less rapidly and thus maintain in-service illumination at a higher value than do unventilated units.

ALUMINUM TROFFER WITH EXTRA-HIGH OUTPUT LAMP

Due to high lamp efficiency, long life, low luminance, and good color quality, these lighting fixtures make good industrial light sources except in high narrow areas where low system efficiency will be encountered. This type of lighting fixture is direct, and is shown in Figure 3-8.

Aluminum troffers produce illumination efficiently on the usual working plane. This efficiency, however, is frequently at the expense of quality factors such as shadows and both direct and reflected glare. Shadows, for example, may be disturbing unless the lighting fixtures have a large area or are closely spaced. Glare and reflected glare can be unsatisfactory because of high luminance difference between the source and the darker ceiling and upper walls. Reflected glare can be a problem if luminances visible from below, such as light sources through a cellular louver, are high enough to produce annoying reflections from specular surfaces at the working plane.

COEFFICIENTS OF UTILIZATION

LUMINAIRE	DISTRIBUTION	Spacing Not to Exceed
Category V 2 T-12 Lamps—430 MA Prismatic Lens 2' Wide— For T-10 Lamps—C.U. x 1.01	0 ←—	—→ 180	1.2 x Mounting Height

Reflectances

Ceiling Cavity	80%			50%			10%			0%
Walls	50%	30%	10%	50%	30%	10%	50%	30%	10%	0%
RCR	Coefficients of Utilization									
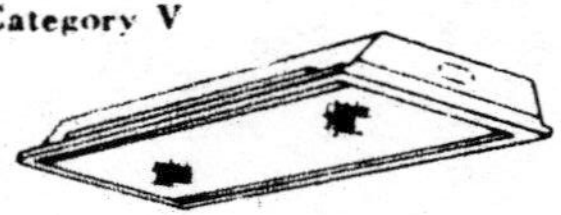 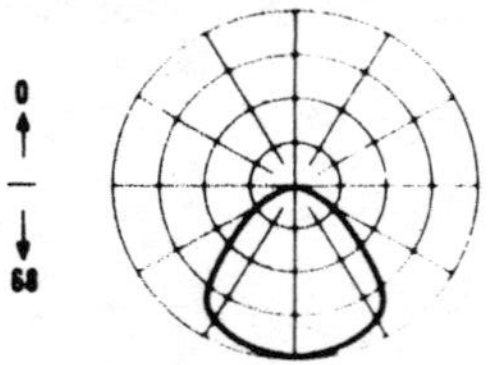 1	.73	.71	.68	.69	.67	.66	.64	.62	.61	.60
2	.66	.62	.59	.62	.59	.57	.58	.56	.55	.53
3	.59	.55	.51	.56	.53	.50	.53	.50	.48	.47
4	.53	.48	.45	.51	.47	.44	.48	.45	.43	.41
5	.48	.43	.39	.46	.42	.39	.44	.40	.38	.36
6	.44	.38	.34	.42	.37	.34	.40	.36	.33	.32
7	.39	.34	.30	.38	.33	.30	.36	.32	.30	.28
8	.36	.31	.26	.34	.30	.26	.33	.29	.26	.25
9	.32	.27	.23	.31	.26	.23	.29	.25	.23	.21
10	.29	.24	.20	.28	.23	.20	.27	.23	.20	.19

Fig. 3–8. Aluminum troffer.

SUSPENDED FIXTURE WITH LUMINOUS BOTTOM

Figure 3-9 shows that this is semiindirect; that is, 60 to 90% of the light output of the lighting fixture is directed toward the ceiling at angles above the horizontal, while the balance is directed downward. The suspended fixture with luminous bottom has most of the advantages of the indirect types, but it is slightly more efficient and it is sometimes preferred to achieve a desirable luminance ratio between the ceiling and luminaire in high-level installations. The diffusing medium employed in this type of luminaire is glass or plastic of a lower density than that employed in indirect equipment.

This type of fixture is usually employed in commerce where the lighting levels never exceed 50 footcandles. When these fixtures are used, their purpose is to make the environment more pleasant, to relieve the contrast between the ceiling and the sales- or display-lighting luminaires, and to soften the shadows produced by such units. High levels of indirect lighting are usually unsatisfactory because of the flat, uninteresting effect created, and therefore an indirect system should never be used alone in store lighting.

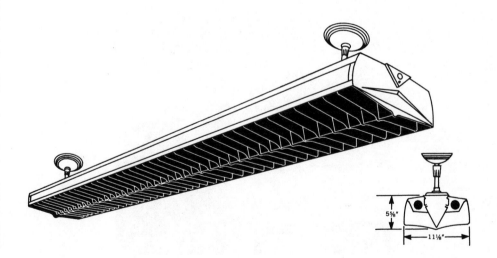

Fig. 3-9. Suspended fixture with luminous bottom.

FLUORESCENT FIXTURE WITH PRISMATIC BOTTOM AND SIDES

This is a semidirect, diffused type of fluorescent lighting fixture with an open top so that approximately 33% of the light is directed upward. Forty to 60% of the light is directed downward at angles below the horizontal. The major portion of the illumination produced on ordinary working planes is a result of the light coming directly from the lighting fixtures. There is, however, a substantial portion of the light directed to the ceiling and side walls. Where these are light in color, the upward light, in addition to supplying a substantial indirect component which adds materially to the diffuse character of the illumination, provides a brighter background against which to view the luminaire. The enclosing diffuser on this fixture distributes light nearly uniformly in all directions.

PRISMATIC WRAPAROUND DIFFUSER

Another type of semi- (almost) direct type luminaire that finds much use in office buildings and other commercial applications. In some

Fig. 3–10. Prismatic wraparound diffuser.

commercial applications, this type of lighting fixture provides nearly all of the general illumination (Figure 3-10). There is little variation except for emphasis on certain displays and high-productivity areas in stores that use this type of lighting system. Such stores rely heavily on this type of lighting and ordinarily require from 100 to 200 foot-candles. Department stores, however, use moderate levels of direct general lighting and depend more on super-imposed sales and display area lighting.

TROFFER WITH PLASTIC LOUVER

A strict direct type of fluorescent fixture used quite extensively in commerce and industry (Figure 3-11). In industry—where uniform illumination throughout an area is not a necessity—this type of lighting fixture can be positioned with specific reference to various working points. The fixture should, however, supply sufficient light for all necessary purposes in aisleways and for the maintenance of satisfactory luminance ratios throughout the room (Figure 3-12).

Fig. 3-11. Troffer with plastic louver.

Fig. 3–12. Application of the fixture shown in Figure 3–11.

FIXTURE WITH DROPPED WHITE DIFFUSER

A direct lighting fixture that provides high-quality, glare-free light for commercial (especially office buildings and food stores) and some industrial applications.

In very large offices, the luminance from these fixtures is especially important because of the large number of lighting fixtures that fall within the normal field of view. Furthermore, since there is often no predominant line of sight, the luminaires should be of acceptable luminance when viewed from any direction. With such equipment, the positioning of the lighting fixtures is not critical as long as they are spaced to give uniform distribution of light throughout the room. In large offices where desks are placed against the wall, additional lighting fixtures should be provided near the wall to keep the illumination up to room average. Whenever there is a predominating line of sight, the lighting fixtures should be oriented to take advantage of their lowest luminances and smallest luminous areas.

STRIP LIGHTING IN COVES

Cove lighting has long been used for decorative and as an indirect light source. The cove lighting detail in Figure 3–13 shows bare (strip) fluorescent lighting fixtures mounted with one edge of the fixture 4 inches from the wall and the other edge flush with the mounting board. To provide a warm, social atmosphere, deluxe warm-white lamps should be used. This type of lamp is also more flattering to people's complexions than are cool-white lamps.

Valance and cornice lighting fall into the same category as cove

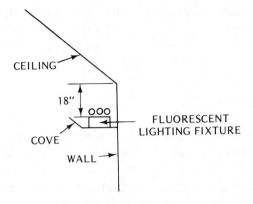

Fig. 3-13. Cove lighting detail.

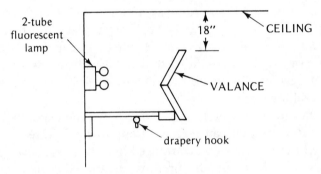

Fig. 3-14. Valance lighting.

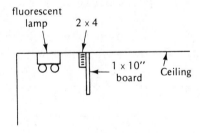

Fig. 3-15. Cornice lighting.

lighting. While either cornice or valance lighting adds life to draperies or walls, both will also supplement the general room lighting level. Valances are nearly always used at windows, usually with draperies. They provide uplight, which reflects off the ceiling for general room illumination, and also down-light, for drapery accent (Figure 3-14).

Cornice lighting directs all light downward to give dramatic interest to wall coverings, draperies, and the like; this type of lighting is especially suited for rooms with low ceilings. Figure 3–15 gives construction details for a typical cornice lighting arrangement.

LUMINOUS CEILINGS

The ideal general lighting system for a residential kitchen and bathroom is a luminous ceiling. This arrangement provides a "skylight" effect, which greatly reduces eye strain and makes seeing easier. A dimming control can be added for even greater versatility.

To determine the number of 4–foot, 40–watt fluorescent lamps that will be required to properly illuminate a residential kitchen or bathroom, divide the total ceiling area by 8 square feet. For example, let's assume that a kitchen is 14 feet by 10 feet for a total area of (14 X 10 = 140) 140 square feet. Divide this figure by 8 square feet for an answer of 17.5 (rounded to 18) 40–watt lamps—the number required to evenly illuminate the ceiling panels to the recommended lighting level for kitchens.

Since the kitchen in question is 14 feet long, the maximum number of 4–foot fixtures that can be placed end-to-end is three. Therefore, the 18 fixtures will have to be arranged in 6 rows, as shown in Figure 3–16. However, these same fixtures may be turned at right angles and spaced as shown in Figure 3–17—a somewhat better arrangement since there is less "dead space" between the ends of the fixtures and the walls.

Luminous ceilings are also used extensively in high-quality commercial installations. The following information is provided for a

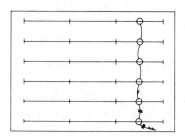

Fig. 3–16. Arrangement of the lighting fixtures for the area described in the text.

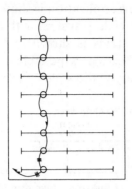

Fig. 3–17. A somewhat better arrangement for the kitchen lighting plan.

typical department store application with an approximate area of 45,000 square feet.

Room cavity depth	7'6"
Room cavity ratio	1.1
Ceiling reflectance	80%
Wall reflectance	50%
Floor reflectance	20%
Room area	4,512 sq ft
Ceiling height (varies)	9'6" to 11'0"
Lumens per lamp	3,100
Maintenance factor	75%
Number of lamps	414
Coefficient of utilization	50%
Initial footcandles	141
Maintained footcandles	106

1. Light dimensions from center to center varied from 4'6" to 5'6" to eliminate the shadows on the ceiling caused by ducts and other obstacles.
2. Also, in some areas, a single strip of lights was installed on the ducts to eliminate shadows.
3. The height of the illuminated ceiling varied from 9'6" to 11'0".
4. The ceiling cavity depth of 2'6" was constant throughout the building.
5. The lamps used were twin-lamp, 4-foot, 40–watt cool-white fluorescents.

A sectional view of this application is shown in Figure 3-18.

A unique illuminated ceiling system with advantages not normally possible with regular systems is shown in Figure 3-19. Because of the indirect lighting effect, it is possible to achieve a very evenly lighted ceiling, using a very shallow plenum space from 6 to 12 inches.

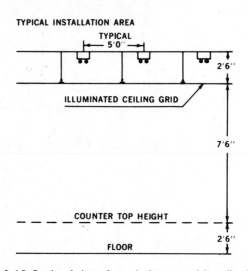

Fig. 3-18. Sectional view of a typical commercial application.

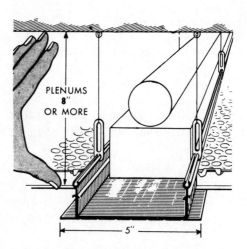

Fig. 3-19. Because of this system's indirect lighting effect, it is possible to achieve a very evenly lighted ceiling, using a very shallow plenum space from 6 to 12 inches.

A sturdy extruded aluminum channel acts as the main support track with standard fluorescent strip fixtures mounted in an inverted position inside the main track, subsequently suspended a short distance below a standard acoustical or plaster ceiling. Standard lamp spacing of 28, 34, 40 and 52 inches give lighting levels up to 75 footcandles using continuously mounted single-lamp, 430–MA fixtures.

EFFECT OF HUMIDITY ON FLUORESCENT LAMPS

The electrostatic charge on the outside of a fluorescent lamp bulb effects the voltage required to start the arc. Humid air surrounding the lamp can form a film of moisture on the bulb which affects this surface charge and makes necessary much higher starting voltages. Lamps used on instant-start and rapid-start circuits are made with an invisible outside silicone coating which disperses the moisture film and ensures reliable starting under all conditions of humidity. In a preheat-type of circuit, the starting voltage pulse is sufficient to strike the arc even at high humidities.

EFFECT OF VOLTAGE

The voltage at the luminaire should be kept well within the normal operating range for the ballast. Low voltage, as well as high voltage, reduces efficiency and shortens lamp life. This is in contrast with

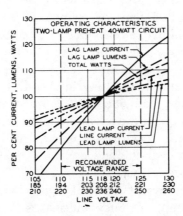

Fig. 3–20. Operating characteristics for a two-lamp preheat 40–watt circuit.

filament lamps, where low voltage reduces efficiency but prolongs life. Low voltage may also cause starting difficulty. Slow or delayed starting results in a more rapid wasting away of emission material, and consequently in shortened lamp life. On voltages above the specified range, the operating current becomes excessive and may not only overheat the ballast, but cause premature end-blackening and early lamp failure. The normal operating range for "low-voltage" ballasts is 110 to 125 volts, for "high-voltage" equipment 220 to 250 volts (Figure 3–20).

A large "dip" or reduction in line voltage will affect the stability of the arc. The voltage reduction that a lamp will withstand without extinguishing depends on the lamp type and the ballast characteristics. For 40–watt T–12 lamps in various types of circuits the line voltage can drop to the following values before the lamps will go out:

Preheat	Approximately 75% of normal volts
Rapid-start series-sequence	Approximately 80% of normal volts
Instant-start lead-lag	Approximately 60% of normal volts
Instant-start series-sequence	Approximately 50% of normal volts

EFFECT OF FREQUENCY

The current-limiting characteristics of a ballast depend directly on the frequency of the power supply, and for this reason ballasts must be used only on the frequency for which they were designed. With a frequency lower than design, for example a 60–cycle ballast on a 50–cycle supply, the inductive reactance of a lag ballast is reduced, and higher current flows through the lamp, resulting in shorter lamp life and an overheated ballast. On a frequency higher than design, the lamp current is reduced, resulting in shorter lamp life and lowered light output. On the lead side of a lead-lag ballast these effects are reversed: lower frequency decreases current, and higher frequency increases it. Installations at low frequencies, such as 25 cycles, require larger less efficient ballasts, and are more likely to have problems involving stroboscopic effect.

Operation of fluorescent lamps at higher frequencies, such as 400 cycles, increases lamp efficiency and makes possible reduced ballast size, weight, and wattage loss. Practical utilization of these advantages is dependent upon the development of efficient and economical equipment to produce these frequencies.

DIRECT-CURRENT OPERATION

Although the fluorescent lamp is basically an alternating current (ac) lamp, it is adaptable to operation on direct current (dc) provided sufficiently high voltage is available, and the proper auxiliary equipment is used. An external resistance in series with the lamp controls the current. Because of the lack of a voltage peak, lamp starting on dc is more difficult than on ac, and special starting devices such as thermal-type or manual switches, plus starting inductances, are necessary. Although total light output on dc is comparable to that obtained on ac, the greater wattage loss in the resistance reduces the overall lumens per watt efficiency of the dc system to about 60% of that of the ac system. Lamp life is also adversely affected by dc operation, and lamps can be expected to give only about 80% of their normal life.

The steady flow of dc in one direction forces the mercury molecules to one end of the tube, resulting in inadequate generation of the ultraviolet energy required for the fluorescence of the phosphors at the other end. Thus, after a few hours' operation on dc, one end of the lamp may become dim. It is recommended that polarity-reversing switches be installed in dc circuits for all lamps of 30 watts and over, so that the direction of the current flow can be reversed when necessary.

BRIGHTNESS

The brightness of fluorescent lamps varies with bulb diameter and current loading. However, all fluorescent lamps are low-brightness sources compared with filament and mercury lamps, because the surface over which the light is generated is so much larger.

STROBOSCOPIC EFFECT

Some variation in light output with the cycle variation of the current is characteristic of all light sources operated on ac. The filament of an incandescent lamp retains enough heat so that its drop in light output at the point of zero current flow is not noticeable, except occasionally when low-wattage lamps are operated on a 25–cycle supply. With fluorescent lamps the arc is completely extinguished twice during each cycle, and the carry-over of light is dependent on the phosphorescent qualities of the coating. This characteristic of the phosphors varies considerably. The phosphor used in the green lamp has the greatest carry-over while that used in the blue lamp has the least. The type of circuit on which the lamps are operated also influences the degree and nature of the light output variation.

Rapid fluctuations of a light source may result in stroboscopic effect, the tendency to see moving objects in repetitive flashes at successive positions. In an unusual combination of circumstances where this might be a problem, lead-lag ballasts will reduce stroboscopic effect because the two lamps are operating out of phase, and will reach their maximum light outputs at different instants. Where further reduction is necessary, operation of lamps on separate phases of a three-phase system will result in a freedom from flicker comparable to that of most filament lamps.

COOLNESS

The fluorescent lamp, primarily because of its higher efficacy, produces light with considerably less accompanying heat than the filament lamp. The total heat developed by any light source is in direct proportion to its energy consumption (one watt-hour of power consumed produces 3.414 Btus of heat), and fluorescent lamps emit two to three times as much light as filament lamps of the same wattage while generating the same amount of heat.

A further difference between the two types of lamps is the form which the heat takes. Not only does the fluorescent lamp produce less total heat for a given amount of light, but less than one-half of the heat it does produce is in the form of radiant energy (radiated heat plus light), whereas about three-quarters of the heat from a filament lamp is radiant energy. Thus, for equal light output the radiant heat generated by fluorescent lamps is approximately one-fifth of that produced by filament lamps. Conducted and convected heat, which accounts for the balance of the total energy, is chiefly dissipated upward, and contributes much less to the sensation of heat derived from the lighting installation.

LUMINANCES OF COOL WHITE FLUORESCENT LAMPS			
Lamp Type	Approx. Candelas per Sq. In.	Lamp Type	Approx. Candelas per Sq. In.
Preheat		**SUPER-HI**	
4-W T-5 6″	5.1	48″ T-12 110-W	11.5
6-W T-5 9″	6.9	72″ T-12 160-W	11.5
8-W T-5 12″	7.4	96″ T-12 215-W	11.5
13-W T-5 21″	7.0		
14-W T-12 15″	3.5	**Circline**	
15-W T-8 18″	5.5	22-W T-9 8¼″ Diam.	4.8
15-W T-12 18″	3.3	32-W T-10 12″ Diam.	5.0
20-W T-12 24″	3.5	40-W T-10 16″ Diam.	5.2
25-W T-12 33″	3.9		
30-W T-8 36″	6.5	**Instant-Start**	
90-W T-17 60″	5.2	40-W T-12 48″	4.3
		40-W T-17 60″	2.4
Rapid Start			
40-W T-12 48″	4.5	**Slimline**	
30-W T-12 36″	4.2	42″ T-6 25-W	6.1
		64″ T-6 37-W	6.0
High Output		72″ T-8 37.5-W	4.1
24″ T-12 30-W	5.6	96″ T-8 50-W	4.4
48″ T-12 60-W	6.0	48″ T-12 38.5-W	4.2
72″ T-12 85-W	6.1	72″ T-12 56-W	4.2
96″ T-12 110-W	6.2	96″ T-12 73.5-W	4.2

Fig. 3–21. Luminances of cool white fluorescent lamps.

Where total heat is a consideration, as for instance in the computation of air-conditioning load, the quantity that is important is of course total lamp wattage, rather than radiant heat. It is also necessary to add to the lamp wattage the watts consumed by any ballasts located within the area in question.

RADIO INTERFERENCE

The mercury arc of a fluorescent lamp causes a sparking action on the lamp electrodes which sets up a series of low-power radio waves. These waves are picked up by radio receiving sets, and may cause interference in the form of a buzzing sound. The noise is generally heard only between stations on the dial, but it may also be noticeable over the entire broadcast band. Interference from fluorescent lamps can readily be identified by tuning the set to a point where the interference is most pronounced, and by then turning off the lamps. If the noise persists, it is of course from some source other than the lamps. Radiation from fluorescent lamps may reach the radio in three ways: by direct radiation from the lamp to the radio aerial circuit, by line radiation from the electric supply to the aerial circuit, and by line feedback from the lamp through the power line to the radio.

Most radio interference from preheat lamps is eliminated by the small condenser ordinarily mounted in the starter-switch container. Manual starting switches should also be provided with suitable condensers having the following minimum values: 0.005 microfarad for 14-, 15-, 20-, 25-, 30-, and 40-watt lamps, 0.010 microfarad for 90-watt lamps. With rapid-start and instant-start systems the condenser is mounted in the ballast.

If further measures prove to be necessary, radio-interference filters (they are commercially available) will give excellent results when properly installed. The simplest of these is a three-section delta-connected capacitor that is grounded to the fixture and connected across the supply lines as they enter the fixture, as close to the lamps as possible. A larger inductive-capacitor filter is also available for installations in laboratories, radio repair shops, rural homes, and other places where conditions are not favorable for good radio reception.

Direct radiation from the lamp diminishes rapidly as the radio aerial is separated from the lamp. If the radio and aerial are at least nine feet from the lamp, interference by direct radiation is negligible.

In rural areas, and in places where radio station signal strength is weak, it may be necessary to take the following additional precautions:

1. Connect the aerial to the radio by a shielded lead-in wire with the shield grounded, or install a "doublet" type aerial with twisted-pair leads.
2. Provide a good radio-frequency ground for the radio.
3. Place the aerial itself out of bulb- and line-radiation range.
4. Use an outside aerial to provide a strong radio signal.
5. Attach a large mesh metal screen to bottom of fixture and ground through the fixture.

NOISE

With any reactor or transformer, some audible frequencies, or *hum*, generated by the alternating magnetic forces are inevitable. Well-made fluorescent auxiliaries and fixtures are now designed to reduce hum to a point where it is rarely objectionable. The degree of ballast noise that is acceptable of course varies with the application. Hum is seldom noticeable in factory spaces or other moderately noisy areas, but it may become annoying in quiet rooms, particularly if the ballast is very close to the user, or if there are a large number of ballasts. Under extreme conditions it may be necessary to locate auxilaries at a remote point, or in soundproof cases.

DIMMING AND FLASHING

Rapid-start lamps can be readily dimmed and flashed when operated on ballasts and circuits specifically designed for these applications.

Dimming ballasts and circuits permit full control of lamp output from full luminance to nearly blackout. Normal dimming service does not adversely affect lamp life. Normal flashing operation (one-half of a second to five seconds burning time) does not materially affect rated lamp life, but long flashing cycles—for example, two minutes on and two minutes off—can increase end discoloration and reduce lamp life.

Chapter 4

Lighting with HID Lamps

HID (high-intensity discharge) *lamps* is a generic term which describes a wide variety of lighting sources. All types of HID lamps consist of gaseous discharge arc tubes which, in the versions designed for lighting, operate at pressures and current densities sufficient to generate desired quantities of radiation within their arcs alone.

Mercury vapor lamps contain arc tubes which are formed of fused quartz. This has resulted in great improvements in lamp life and maintenance of output through life. These arcs radiate ultraviolet energy as well as light, but the glass used in outer bulbs is generally of a heat-resisting type that absorbs most of the ultraviolet. Some mercury lamps have outer bulbs that are internally coated with fluorescent materials which, when activated by the ultraviolet, emit visible energy at wavelengths that modify the color of light from the arc. The General Electric deluxe white mercury lamps, for example, have color characteristics that are well suited to many commercial lighting applications that could not, until recently, have been considered for mercury. General lighting mercury lamps are available in wattages from 50 to 3000 watts.

Multivapor lamps generate light with more than half again the efficiency of the mercury arc, and with better color quality.

In 1965, General Electric introduced the Lucalox lamp, which has the highest light-producing efficiency of any commercial source of white light. This lamp was made possible by the invention of a Lucalox ceramic in a combination that could withstand temperatures and corrosive effects produced by intensely hot vapors of the alkaline metals. The arc consists principally of metallic sodium that yields much better color quality and compactness, and with substantially higher luminous efficacy than has been available before for white light.

84

The outer bulbs of high intensity discharge lamps are designed to provide, as nearly as possible, optimum internal environments for arc-tube performance. For example, the rounded shapes labeled E and BT in Figure 4–1 were devised to maintain uniform temperatures of the bulb walls for better performance of phosphor coatings. The E-bulb improves manufacturing efficiency and eliminates the clear bulb-end on phosphor-lined bulbs.

In some cases, special considerations dictate the bulb shape. The R and PAR contours have been selected to achieve desired directional distribution of light. Some of the smaller T-bulbs are made of highly specialized glasses which are more economically formed in these simple contours.

Most of the general contours of high-intensity discharge lamps are shown in Figure 4–1, which includes verbal descriptions of the code used for the shapes.

Fig. 4–1. The rounded shaped bulbs labeled E and BT were devised to maintain uniform temperatures of the bulb walls for better performance of phosphor coatings.

MERCURY LAMPS

A typical mercury lamp consists of the parts schematically illustrated in Figure 4-2. These components are enclosed in an outer bulb made of borosilicate glass that can withstand high temperatures and that is resistant to thermal shocks like those caused by cold raindrops striking a hot bulb. The outer bulb contains a small quanitity of nitrogen, an inert gas; this atmosphere maintains internal electrical stability, provides thermal insulation for the arc tube, and protects the metal parts from oxidation. The quartz arc tube contains a small quantity of high-purity mercury and a starting gas, argon.

Most mercury lamps operate on ac circuits, and the ac-circuit ballast usually consists of a transformer to convert the distribution voltage of the lighting circuit to the required starting voltage for the lamp, and inductive or capacitive reactance components to control lamp current and—in some ballasts—to improve power factor.

The majority of mercury lamps start and operate equally well in any burning position. However, light output and maintenance of output through the lamp's life are generally slightly higher with vertical than with horizontal operation.

The operating life of mercury lamps is very long, which accounts for much of their popularity in recent years. Most general lighting lamps of 100 to 1000 watts have rated lives in excess of 24,000 hours, while the 50-, 75-, and 100-watt lamps with medium screw bases are rated at 10,000 hours. Ratings are based on operation with properly designed ballasts, with five or more burning hours per start. More frequent starting may reduce life somewhat.

MULTIVAPOR LAMPS

Multivapor lamps are quite similar in physical appearance to conventional clear mercury lamps. The major differences in internal con-

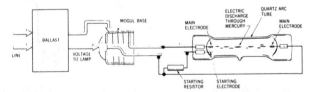

Fig. 4-2. Basic components of a mercury lamp.

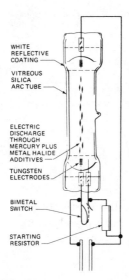

WHITE
REFLECTIVE
COATING

VITREOUS
SILICA
ARC TUBE

ELECTRIC
DISCHARGE
THROUGH
MERCURY PLUS
METAL HALIDE
ADDITIVES

TUNGSTEN
ELECTRODES

BIMETAL
SWITCH

STARTING
RESISTOR

Fig. 4-3. Basic components of a multivapor lamp.

struction and appearance can be seen by comparing the sketch in
Figure 4-3 to the one in Figure 4-2. At present time, two sizes of
multivapor lamps are available: 400 watts and 1000 watts. The 1000-
watt size has been used most widely, largely because of its capability
for delivering so much light from a single lighting fixture. Applications
for multivapor include industrial lighting, street lighting, building
floodlighting, and the floodlighting of several major stadiums to
provide the amount of color quality of light needed for color tele-
casts, without resort to huge increases in power requirements.

LUCALOX LAMPS

The construction, operation and radiation characterists of Lucalox
lamps are quite unlike those of the other HID lamps. As the sketch
in Figure 4-4 indicates, the essential internal components are fewer.
The sketch cannot, however, indicate the tremendous steps in material and processing technology that made this simplification possible.
The result has been the most efficient source of white light ever
made. The two wattages of Lucalox lamps available at the time of
this writing are 275 and 400; they produce light with an efficacy of
100 and 115 lumens per watt (lm/W), respectively. This compares

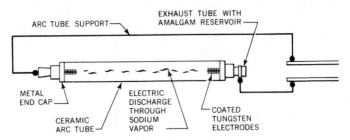

Fig. 4-4. The essential internal components of a Lucalox lamp are fewer as compared to other HID lamps.

with values of about 80 lm/W for fluorescent, 50 lm/W for mercury, and only 15–20 lm/W for incandescent in the types used in commercial and industrial lighting.

CLEAR HID LAMP WITH GLASS REFRACTOR ABOVE PLASTIC LENS

This type of fixture is used in gyms and other high bay areas where a high level of illumination is required; there is also a savings in energy.

NARROW DISTRIBUTION VENTILATED REFLECTOR

In high bay areas of industrial buildings, the work to be done commonly involves rather large three-dimensional objects that have diffuse reflecting characteristics. Under these circumstances, the seeing task is not severe and reflected glare presents no problem.

For these applications, a light source similar to that shown in Figure 4–5 that has a high lumen output is desirable. Such sources in direct reflectors produce light with a directional component that causes slight shadows and mild highlights that aid in seeing. Mercury lamps are usually the most economical sources for high bay lighting. In most cases, a few filament lamps are added to the mercury installations to provide some light that will be available immediately following an electric service interruption. The nature of the work being performed and the reliability of the electric service govern the necessity of installing filament lamps for this purpose.

COEFFICIENTS OF UTILIZATION

Category III — 18" Ventilated Alum. High Bay Conc. Dist. 400-W Clear Vapor Lamp
Spacing Not to Exceed: .7 x Mounting Height

Ceiling Cavity	80%			70%			50%			10%
Walls → RCR	50%	30%	10%	50%	30%	10%	50%	30%	10%	10%
1	.93	.90	.88	.85	.83	.82	.76	.75	.74	.72
2	.86	.82	.79	.79	.77	.74	.72	.70	.69	.67
3	.79	.75	.71	.74	.70	.68	.68	.65	.64	.62
4	.74	.69	.65	.69	.65	.62	.64	.61	.59	.57
5	.68	.63	.59	.64	.60	.57	.60	.57	.54	.53
6	.63	.58	.54	.60	.56	.52	.56	.53	.51	.49
7	.59	.53	.49	.56	.51	.48	.52	.49	.46	.45
8	.55	.49	.45	.52	.47	.44	.49	.46	.43	.41
9	.50	.45	.41	.48	.43	.40	.45	.42	.39	.38
10	.47	.41	.38	.45	.40	.36	.42	.38	.36	.35

Fig. 4–5. Narrow distribution ventilated reflector.

Category III — 18" Ventilated Alum. High Bay Spread Dist. 400-W Coated Vapor Lamp
Spacing Not to Exceed: 1.2 x Mounting Height

Ceiling Cavity	80%			70%			50%			10%
Walls → RCR	50%	30%	10%	50%	30%	10%	50%	30%	10%	10%
1	.88	.86	.81	.80	.79	.77	.71	.70	.69	.67
2	.81	.77	.71	.75	.72	.70	.67	.65	.62	.62
3	.74	.70	.66	.69	.65	.62	.62	.60	.58	.56
4	.68	.63	.59	.64	.60	.57	.58	.55	.51	.51
5	.63	.57	.53	.60	.55	.51	.54	.51	.47	.47
6	.58	.52	.48	.55	.50	.46	.50	.46	.43	.43
7	.53	.47	.42	.51	.45	.41	.46	.43	.40	.39
8	.48	.43	.39	.46	.41	.37	.42	.39	.36	.35
9	.44	.39	.35	.42	.37	.34	.39	.36	.33	.31
10	.41	.35	.31	.39	.34	.30	.36	.32	.30	.28

Fig. 4–6. Intermediate distribution ventilated reflector.

Category III — 24" Ventilated Porcelain Enamel 1000-W Phosphor Coated Vapor Lamp
Spacing Not to Exceed: 1.3 x Mounting Height

Ceiling Cavity	80%			70%			50%			10%
Walls → RCR	50%	30%	10%	50%	30%	10%	50%	30%	10%	10%
1	.86	.83	.80	.78	.76	.73	.68	.67	.65	.63
2	.77	.72	.68	.70	.66	.63	.61	.59	.57	.55
3	.68	.62	.57	.62	.58	.51	.55	.49	.49	.47
4	.61	.55	.49	.56	.51	.47	.50	.46	.43	.41
5	.55	.48	.42	.50	.45	.41	.45	.41	.38	.36
6	.49	.42	.37	.45	.39	.35	.40	.36	.33	.31
7	.43	.39	.31	.39	.34	.30	.36	.31	.28	.26
8	.39	.32	.28	.34	.30	.26	.32	.28	.25	.23
9	.35	.28	.24	.30	.27	.23	.29	.25	.22	.20
10	.32	.25	.21	.27	.24	.20	.26	.22	.19	.17

Fig. 4–7. Wide distribution ventilated reflector.

INTERMEDIATE DISTRIBUTION VENTILATED REFLECTOR

This type of lighting fixture (Figure 4–6) is best suited for use in high narrow rooms where it is necessary and more economical to produce illumination on the horizontal plane. Where the seeing task is inclined at an angle exceeding approximately 45°, lighting fixtures with a spread or widespread distribution should be used as shown in Figure 4–7, even though somewhat less light reaches the horizontal plane.

WIDE DISTRIBUTION VENTILATED REFLECTOR

In wide high bay areas, lighting fixtures with a wide distribution (Figure 4–8) provide greater overlapping of light beams than is economical in narrow rooms, with resulting reduction in shadow intensity and higher vertical surface illumination. In rows of lighting fixtures near the walls, narrower distribution equipment may be used to minimize loss through wall and window absorption.

FLOOD LIGHTS

Floodlight equipment is divided into seven types according to beam spread, the angle between the two directions in which the candle-power is 10% of the maximum candlepower which is at or near the center of the beam. Table 4–1 shows the seven types of available floodlight equipment.

Although the choice of beam spread for a particular application depends upon individual circumstances, the following general principles apply:

1. The greater the distance from the floodlight to the area to be lighted, the narrower the beam spread desired.

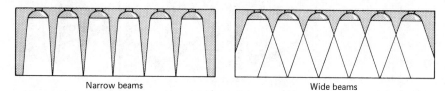

Narrow beams   Wide beams

Fig. 4–8. Wide distribution units provide greater overlapping of light beams.

Table 4-1

OUTDOOR FLOODLIGHT LUMINAIRE DESIGNATIONS*						
		Minimum Efficiencies (per cent)				
Beam Spread Degrees	NEMA Type	Incandescent Lamps		Mercury Lamps		Fluo-rescent Lamps
		Effective Reflector Area (square inches)				
		Under 227	Over 227	Under 227	Over 227	Any
10 up to 18	1	34	35	..	..	20
18 up to 29	2	36	36	22	30	25
29 up to 46	3	39	45	24	34	35
46 up to 70	4	42	50	35	38	42
70 up to 100	5	46	50	38	42	50
100 up to 130	6	..	..	42	46	55
130 and up	7	..	..	46	50	55

2. Since, by definition, the candlepower at the edge of a flood-light beam is 10% of the candlepower near the center of the beam, the illumination level at the edge of the beam is one-tenth or less of that at the center. To obtain reasonable uniformity of illumination, the beams of individual floodlights must overlap each other as well as the edge of the surface to be lighted.

3. The percentage of beam lumens falling outside the area to be lighted is usually lower with narrow-beam units than it is with wide-beam units. Thus narrow-beam units are preferable where they will provide the necessary degree of uniformity of illumination and the proper footcandle level.

The location of floodlighting equipment is usually dictated by the type of application and the physical surroundings. If the area is large, individual towers or poles spaced at regular intervals may be required for even lighting; smaller areas may require only one tower with all equipment concentrated on it or adjacent buildings to be used as floodlight locations.

In planning any floodlighting system, it is important that the light be properly controlled. Strong light that is parallel to a highway or railroad track can be a dangerous source of glare to oncoming traffic, and light thrown indiscriminately on adjacent property may be a serious nuisance.

DECORATIVE HID LIGHTING FIXTURES

Recently, HID lighting is finding its place in commercial installations for general illumination. Attractive fixtures and color-improved lamps have been a tremendous factor in this application. For example, modern supermarkets are using mercury lamps in recessed fixtures for general illumination with a few incandescent lamps as standbys in case of a temporary power interruption. A typical example is shown in Figure 4–9.

COLOR

On the basis of color, one manufacturer's mercury lamps are described by the following terms:

Clear mercury—for all types having a clear or frosted outer bulb, without phosphor coating.

Colortone—for all types in which the color is different from that of clear mercury lamps. Thes include all phosphor-coated (mercury fluorescent) lamps and yellow lamps:

Hi-output white—for phosphor coated lamps having a small degree of color correction with an appreciable gain in lumen output as compared with similar clear lamps. Code designation: /W.

Standard white—for phosphor-coated lamps having a considerable degree of color correction at a slight sacrifice in lumen output as compared with similar clear lamps. Code designation: /C.

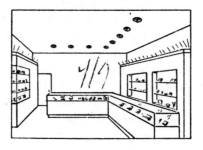

Fig. 4–9. Typical example of decorative HID lighting system.

Deluxe white—for phosphor coated lamps providing best available color rendition in mercury lamps, generally without sacrifice in appreciable initial lumen output, but with some reduction in mean, or maintained lumens. Code designations: /DX.

Yellow—for lamps with yellow bulbs. Code designation: /Y.

AUXILIARY EQUIPMENT

Current-limiting ballasts have been designed for each type of mercury lamp to furnish proper lamp voltage and current ballasting through the inductance of the windings. The electrical characteristics of ballasts, when used in with discharge lamps, are such as to produce a low power factor. This situation is commonly corrected by the addition of capacitance in the form of a condenser, generally built into the ballast. Uncorrected ballasts have power factors of 50 to 60%, whereas the corrected ones achieve 90% or better (Figure 4-10).

Two lamp ballasts only slightly larger than the single-lamp type operate one lamp on a leading current and the other on a lagging current, producing an overall power factor of about 90% and reducing stroboscopic effect. All ballasts must be designed for the specific voltage and frequency of the supply with which they are to be used. For dependable starting and good lamp life, mercury lamps must be operated within rather narrow voltage limits, and the primary of each

NOMINAL ELECTRICAL CHARACTERISTICS OF MERCURY LAMPS							
Electrical Class	Lamp Watts	Open-Circuit RMS Volts ①		② Lamp Starting Current (Amps)	Lamp Operating		③ Ballast Loss, Wattage Range
		50°F	−20°F		Current (Amps)	Volts	
H-45	40 ④	180	180	0.8	0.53	90	7-10
H-46	50	210	210	0.9	0.6	95	10-15
H-43	75	225	225	1.0	0.66	130	10-15
{H44-4 H38-4}	100	225	225	1.3	0.85	130	18-35
H39-22	175	210	225	2.2	1.5	130	30-35
H37-5	250	210	225	3.1	2.1	130	18-42
H33-1	400	210	225	5	3.2	135	25-65
H40-17	425	460	460	2.5	1.7	265	21-25
H35-18	700	460	460	4.2	2.8	265	32-65
H34-12	1000	210	375	12	8.0	135	40-85
H36-15	1000	460	460	6	4	265	40-100
H9	3000	850	...	9.3	6.1	535	135-165

Fig. 4-10. Nominal electrical characteristics of mercury lamps.

ballast is provided with taps for several voltages. Mercury lamps may also be operated from regulate-output (constant-wattage) ballasts or in straight series circuits without individual lamp ballasts, provided power safeguards are applied. Most equipment is designed for a frequency of 60 cycles. Operation on lower frequencies to 25 cycles is possible, although larger ballasts are required and stroboscopic effect is greater. Since the arc is actually extinguished each time the current reverses, at frequencies below 25 cycles the mercury vapor may have time between cycles to deionize and the electrodes to cool sufficiently enough to prevent restriking of the arc.

OPERATING CHARACTERISTICS

Starting and Restarting

In addition to the two operating electrodes, nearly all mercury lamps contain a starting electrode. An electrical field is first set up between the starting electrode and the adjacent main electrode, causing an emission of electrons which develops a local glow and ionizes the starting gas. The arc then starts between the main electrodes, and the mercury gradually becomes vaporized and carries an increasing portion of the current. During this process, the arc stream changes from the diffuse bluish glow characteristic of the argon arc to the blue-green of mercury increasing greatly in brilliance and becoming concentrated in the center of the tube. At the instant the arc strikes, the lamp current is high and the voltage is low. At ordinary room temperatures with no enclosing fixture, normal operating values are reached after a warm-up period of three to four minutes, depending on lamp and ballast type. The single-bulb H9FJ lamp requires approximately seven to ten minutes. During the warm-up, the current drops and the voltage rises until the arc attains a point of stabilization in vapor pressure.

An interruption in the power supply or a sudden voltage drop may extinguish the arc. Most ballasts are designed to permit a voltage drop of 15% without extinguishing the lamp; some types permit 25% or more. Before the lamp will relight, it must cool sufficiently to reduce the vapor pressure to a point where the arc will restrike at the voltage available. For most types of lamps, restriking time (cooling

REFERENCE DATA OF REPRESENTATIVE LIFEGUARD MERCURY LAMPS

ASA Designation	Bulb Shape	Description	Arc Length Approx.	Maximum Over-all Length (inches)	Light Center Length (Inches)	① Approx. Initial Lumens (At 100 Hrs.)	② Approx. Mean Lumens
40 Watts							
H46DL/DX	B-17	Deluxe White	5/8	5 1/8	3 1/8	1260	920
50 Watts							
H46DL/DX	B-17	Deluxe White	5/8	5 1/8	3 1/8	1550	1150
75 Watts							
H43AZ	B-21	Clear	1	6 1/2	3 3/4	2800	2350
H43AY/C	B-21	Standard White	1	6 1/2	3 3/4	2750	2300
H43AY/W	B-21	HI-OUTPUT White	1	6 1/2	3 3/4	2900	2300
H43AY/DX	B-21	Deluxe White	1	6 1/2	3 3/4	2800	2200
100 Watts							
H38-4LL	A-23	Clear	1 1/8	5 7/16	3 1/2	4100	3450
H38-4MP/C	A-23	Standard White	1 1/8	5 7/16	3 1/2	4000	3300
H38-4MP/W	A-23	HI-OUTPUT White	1 1/8	5 7/16	3 1/2	4400	3450
H38-4MP/DX	A-23	Deluxe White	1 1/8	5 7/16	3 1/2	4300	3200
H38-4GS	PAR-38	Clear, Reflector Spot	...	5 7/16	...	2800	1800
H38-4JM	PAR-38	Clear, Reflector Flood	...	5 7/16	...	2800	1800
H38-4HT	BT-25	Clear	1 1/8	7 1/2	5	4100	3450
H38-4JA/C	BT-25	Standard White	1 1/8	7 1/2	5	4100	3400
H38-4JA/W	BT-25	HI-OUTPUT White	1 1/8	7 1/2	5	4400	3550
H38-4JA/DX	BT-25	Deluxe White	1 1/8	7 1/2	5	4400	3300
175 Watts							
H39-22KB	BT-28	Clear	2	8 5/16	5	7700	6600
H39-22KC/C	BT-28	Standard White	2	8 5/16	5	7700	6300
H39-22KC/W	BT-28	HI-OUTPUT White	2	8 5/16	5	8600	6650
H39-22KC/DX	BT-28	Deluxe White	2	8 5/16	5	8500	6800
H39-22BP/DX	R-40	Deluxe White Reflector	2	7 1/2	...	5300	4250
250 Watts							
H37-5KB	BT-28	Clear	2 1/8	8 5/16	5	12100	9850
H37-5KC/DX	BT-28	Deluxe White	2 1/8	8 5/16	5	13000	9750

Fig. 4–11. Reference data of representative lifeguard mercury lamps.

time until the lamp will restart) is approximately the same as warm-up time, although in hot enclosed fixtures it will be slightly longer.

CIRCUIT PROTECTION

The magnitude of the line current to the ballast during the warm-up period varies considerably with the lamp and ballast combination. It may be lower than normal operating line current, or, for some ballast types, as much as 75% greater. In designing the distribution system and circuit protection, the ballast manufacturer should be consulted to ascertain the maximum starting line current for the specific equipment to be used.

APPLICATION INFORMATION

Color

The line spectrum of clear mercury lamps is a very efficient source of light, but its deficiency in red and preponderance of blue and green results in marked distortion of object colors, and makes its use undesirable where the appearance of colors is important. Prior to the advent of the color-corrected lamp, this deficiency was sometimes overcome by adding some incandescent lamps. Partly because of the relatively short life of filament lamps, this procedure was unsatisfactory and it is no longer necessary. Where color rendition is importnat, there is a choice of three kinds of mercury-fluorescent lamps; Deluxe White for best color (most red, least yellow-green), Standard White, or Hi-Output White. Figure 4–12 compares the color and lumen output of these types with those of the clear mercury lamp.

Lamp Type	Initial Approx. Light Output	Approx. Per Cent of Light in Red (600 to 760nm)
Clear Mercury	100 %	1 to 2%
COLORTONE		
HI-OUTPUT White	110%	4 to 7%
Standard White	97%	8 to 13%
Deluxe White	90-102%	13 to 16%

Fig. 4–12. Color and lumen output comparison of mercury-fluorescent lamps and clear mercury lamps.

Semireflector lamps usually have slightly less color correction than do wholly phosphor-coated lamps.

A yellow mercury lamp, the 400W H33-1-GL/y, is available for such special applications as warnings of intersections, underpasses, railroad crossings, etc., and for interesting floodlighting effects.

Stroboscopic Effect

The arc of a mercury lamp operating on a 60-cycle ac is completely extinguished 120 times per second. Thus there is a tendency for the eye to see in flashes, with the result that a rapidly moving object may appear to move in a series of jerks (*stroboscopic effect*). This is often unnoticed, and in most installations it is not a serious disadvantage. Where necessary, stroboscopic effect may be greatly reduced by operating pairs of lamps on lead-lag two-lamp ballasts, or three lamps on separate phases of a three-phase supply. The use of incandescent lamps in combination with mercury lamps also lessens stroboscopic effect.

For industrial applications where high output is more important than color (such as the lighting of steel mills, aircraft plants, and foundries), High-Output White or Standard White semireflector lamps are often the most economical choice, particularly those types that may be operated directly from 460-volt circuits with inexpensive choke-type ballasts (the 100-watt H36-15KY/W and 425-watt H-4017DN/C, for example). Wholly coated lamps have lower surface brightness than do semireflector lamps, and at relatively low mounting heights they may provide a more comfortable lighting installation, as well as better color rendition.

For roadway lighting and floodlighting, choice of lamp size and color depends on the requirements of the particular lighting task. Clear lamps have a better optical effectiveness in most fixtures designed for these purposes, but Colortone lamps are being used increasingly in roadway lighting, and are quite commonly used for the floodlighting of parking areas. The 75-, 100-, 175-, and 250-watt lamps are used for lighting secondary and tertiary streets, the 400-, 700-, and 1000-watt sizes for major streets and highways. Deluxe White lamps of appropriate size are recommended for high-level "white way" lighting.

For commercial and nonindustrial interior applications, such as the lighting of gymnasiums, banks, high-ceilinged offices, transportation terminal buidings, and so forth, Deluxe White lamps are recommended. The Standard White color may be used where economy is more important than color quality. In installations where the unavoidable slight hum created by the ballasts might be objectionable, the ballasts are sometimes located outside of the room.

Chapter 5

Lighting with Combinations

Modern lighting techniques greatly influence the appearance of interior environments and, when a combination of different types of lamps are used, an endless number of moods and effects may be achieved. In some situations, no one light source can be completely satisfactory. For example, for critical color matching, colors which match under one light source may not match under another. Therefore, for the most accurate work, two or more light sources having different light-color characteristics are necessary.

Light-source combinations, such as a combination of incandescent and fluorescent lamps, are also widely used in commercial applications to achieve a particular objective. One example would be the use of incandescent down lights alternated between sections of fluorescent fixtures as shown in Figure 5-1. This figure shows a partial plan view of a unique cove lighting arrangement which was designed to comply with the building owner's desire to have an indirect lighting system. Laminated beams ran the entire width of the building over which a 2-inch thick tongue-and-groove solid wood deck was installed; the bottom or interior side of the deck was painted white for light-reflection purposes. A cove was then constructed on each side of each beam, both of which ran the entire length of the beam. In this cove, alternating fluorescent and incandescent fixtures—as shown in the plan—were utilized. With this arrangement, the fluorescent lighting fixtures provided indirect general illumination by the reflected light off the ceiling. The recessed incandescent fixtures with adjustable lamps provided direct light for highlighting merchandise on the counters directly below the coves (Figure 5-2).

Another important use of light-source combinations is where HID lamps are used because even a momentary power interruption

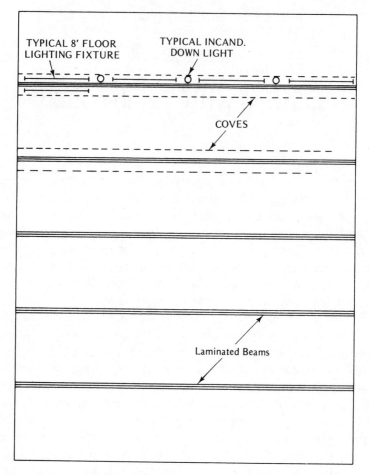

Fig. 5–1. Floor plan of a store building utilizing a combination of fluorescent and incandescent fixtures.

will cause the lamps to go out, and it may be as long as 15 minutes before they will restart and come up to full light output. Therefore, for safety reasons, any HID lighting system for building interiors should be supplemented with another type of light source.

For example, the floor plan of a school recreation area is shown in Figure 5–3. Note that the main light source consists of 15 Type 5 lighting fixtures—each containing a 250–watt color-corrected mercury vapor lamp. Note also that 8 Type 7 lighting fixtures are used to

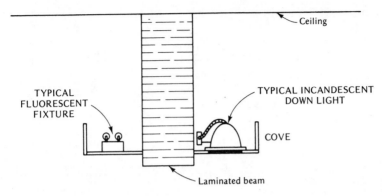

TYPICAL FLUORESCENT FIXTURE

TYPICAL INCANDESCENT DOWN LIGHT

Ceiling

COVE

Laminated beam

Fig. 5–2. Cross-section through one of the beams in Fig. 5–1.

supplement the other fixtures for greater lighting intensity and also to provide a light source should a power interruption occur.

The Type 7 fixtures are controlled by a single-pole switch near one of the doors while the three circuits feeding the fifteen Type 5 fixtures are controlled by a three-pole, 20-amp lighting magnetic contacter.

A combination of different light sources adds greatly to the appearance of merchandise. A deep-pile rug, for example, has a textured finish. Evenly diffused fluorescent light may illuminate each fiber of such a rug so uniformly that it would be difficult to appraise the pattern and depth of the pile. However, if directional incandescent light is used in combination with diffused fluorescent light, the soft texture and deep nap of the rug will be greatly emphasized.

Shadows of various objects are sometimes excessively sharp if only a single light source is used; two or three different light sources with overlapping beams may give better results. In fact, most kinds of merchandise will show up better under a dual system of fluorescent and incandescent lighting than under an all-fluorescent or all-incandescent system.

The space occupied by the show window is the most valuable area in the store, but without good lighting its usefulness as an advertising medium can be almost lost. For the show window to function at optimum efficiency, it must capture the attention and interest of prospective shoppers. Brightness is invaluable in attracting attention, but without inviting, interesting, or dramatic displays

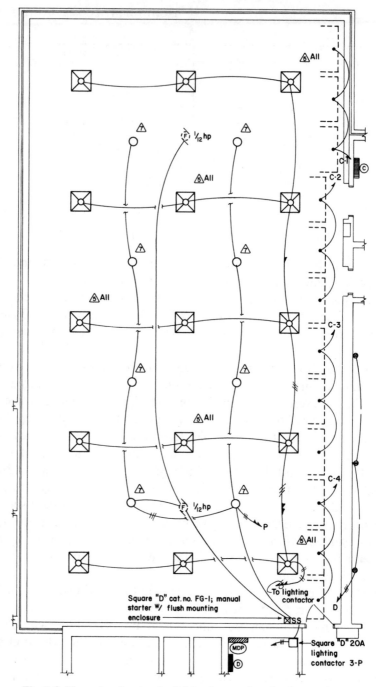

Fig. 5-3. Floor plan showing the lighting layout of a school recreation area.

the window may receive only a glance. On the other hand, an otherwise interesting display may go unnoticed if it is not sufficiently bright. The control of brightness, highlight, and shadow is the key to a successful window display.

Show window lighting equipment should be flexible enough to spotlight a small display vividly, to illuminate a larger area with directional light, or to flood the entire window with nondirectional diffuse light, as from fluorescent luminaires. Many window decorations require a combination of all three systems to display a single item. Dimming devices and flexible switching are valuable assets; colored lens caps for reflector and projector lamps are frequently necessary. (Figure 5–4).

The illumination levels needed in show windows in the daytime are considerably higher than those needed for night lighting. In the daytime, the brightness of the display must be high enough to overcome reflected images of automobiles at the curb, light-colored buildings across the street, and other bright surfaces that may be mirrored by the store window. The typical luminance of such surfaces may be at least 1000 footlamberts. The luminance of the reflected image is then approximately 100 footlamberts, since the specular reflectance of the window is about 10%. A white display having a reflectance of 80% and illuminated to a level of 500 footcandles has a luminance of 400 footlamberts, four times that of the reflected image. Under those conditions the display is visible, although reflected images can still be slightly annoying. The general rule is that in order to "see through" reflected images in the window glass, the displays inside the window must be at least as bright as the reflected images and preferably several times as bright.

Large reflected images that are relatively uniform in brightness, as for instance the sky, raise the apparent brightness of those parts of the display that are in relative shadow, thus tending to destroy contrasts that may have been planned for spectacular effect. Images of isolated bright surfaces such as the sun reflected off automobile chrome cause unnatural highlights on the display and are more confusing and annoying than images of uniform brightness.

For these reasons it is difficult to lay down general rules for illumination levels in show windows. Each window is a special case, and must be studied in relation to its orientation and surroundings.

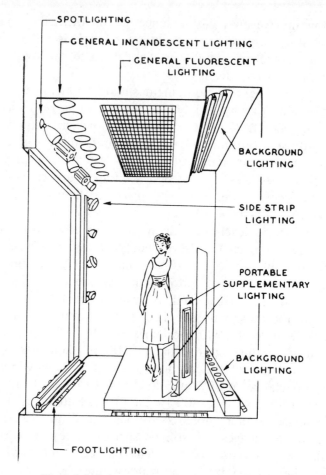

Fig. 5–4. Lighting considerations for a show window.

The problem of overcoming reflected images in store windows is even more troublesome for open-front stores than for stores using conventional windows with a back that obscures the view from the street into the store. For open-front stores the entire interior is the display, and it is obviously impracticable to create sufficiently high brightness to overcome reflected images. The windows may be tilted, or awnings may be utilized effectively.

The lighting flexibility of theater and television lighting can only be accomplished by the use of several different light sources. In general, light sources must be used to produce a quality of light which usually falls within three basic catagories:

1. *Soft light*—diffused lighting that produces infinite margins and poorly defined shadows.
2. *Key light*—lighting with defined margins, producing soft-edged shadows.
3. *Hard light*—lighting that produces sharply defined, geometrically precise shadows.

To achieve the basic lighting requirements for stage and television, several combinations of light sources must be used. Fresnel spotlights, scoops, non-lens luminaires, PAR-luminaires and similar lighting fixtures use incandescent lamps, including tungsten-halogen. Arc lights—the kind that use a carbon arc—are also used in theater and stage, as are HID lamps. A typical stage lighting layout is shown in Figure 5–5.

Multipurpose areas, such as fellowship halls in churches, also require the use of lighting combinations. The floor plan of such an area is shown in Figure 5–6. In this area, a general-lighting system is provided to give adequate, quality illumination for Sunday School classes and similar meetings, a subdued, relaxed mood of lighting for church dinners and social functions, and finally, indirect lighting to enhance architectural and decorative features of the area.

General lighting for the area is provided by twenty-one 300–watt incandescent recessed fixtures, designated as Type Four on the drawing. All of these fixtures are controlled (either separately or in groups) by rheostat dimmers to give an average calculated footcandle range of 0 to over 50 footcandles. This varied range of illumination is adequate, and also provides a good atmosphere for any function held in the area.

The 300–watt IF (inside-frosted) incandescent lamps give good general appearance to furnishings, people, and food. Had cool-white fluorescent tubes been used, all food, and especially meats, would have a very poor appearance.

The nine direct wall-wash lighting fixtures (Type One) located behind the speaker platform to highlight the panelled wall are also recessed incandescent fixtures. Each has a half-ellipsoid reflector,

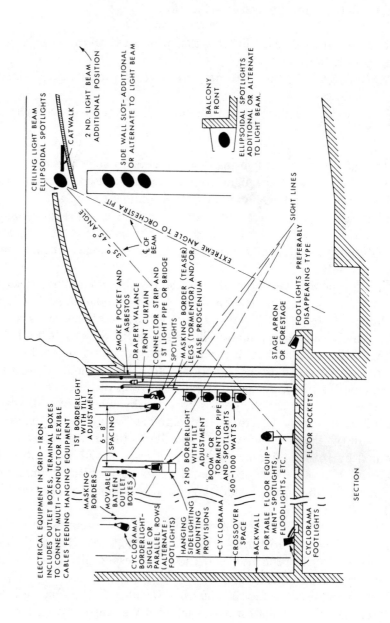

SCHEDULE OF LIGHTING UNITS	
TYPE	WATTAGE
ELLIPSOIDAL SPOTLIGHTS	500-3000
FRESNEL SPOTLIGHTS	500-2000
FOOTLIGHTS	60-100 PER FOOT PER COLOR
BORDERLIGHTS	75-200 PER FOOT PER COLOR
CYCLORAMA BORDERLIGHTS AND FOOTLIGHTS	75-300 PER FOOT PER COLOR
CYCLORAMA FOOTLIGHTS	500-1500
SCENIC PROJECTORS	1000-5000
MISC.	AS REQUIRED

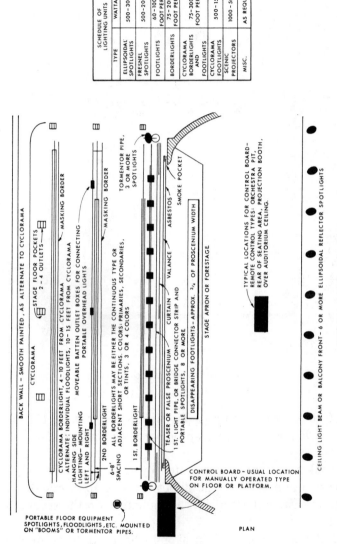

Fig. 5-5. Lighting details for stage lighting.

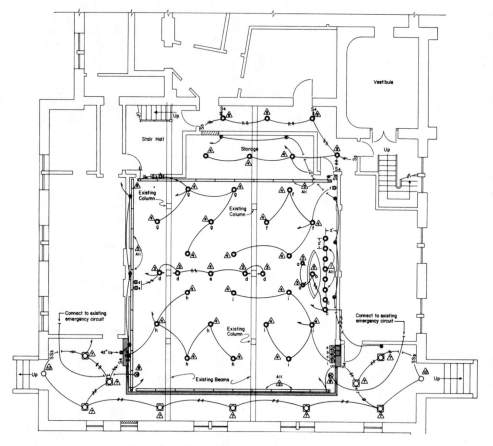

Fig. 5–6. Lighting layout for a church fellowship hall.

a block Coilex baffle, and a rimless scoop trim. Then, 150–watt re-flector-type lamps are used to produce a very nice wall-wash effect without glare.

The speaker is further highlighted by two other recessed fixtures (Type Three) and also by one direct recessed fixture with a 2–inch pinhole lens. The latter provides illumination on the speaker's reading material.

All of the wall-wash and speaker highlight fixtures are also controlled by rheostat dimmers for added effects and versatility. Type Three fixtures are also used to highlight the paneling on the columns located approximately in the center of the area. Continuous rows of 40–watt fluorescent strip lighting are used in coves along the ceiling line on three sides of the area. Each side is controlled by a single-pole toggle switch. These strips of fluorescent lighting provide a supplemental light source for still more versatility in the room lighting, but more important, these additional cove lighting fixtures gives the low ceiling the appearance of being much higher than it actually is.

The floor plan in Figure 5–7 shows the lighting layout for a department store. Recessed, 2' × 4' four-lamp lighting fixtures with acrylic lenses are used throughout the sales area for general lighting. This arrangement provides a uniform lighting level of approximately 65 footcandles throughout the entire area.

Recessed 2' × 4' fluorescent lighting fixtures with 100% acrylic, low-brightness, prismatic lenses are used in the office area to maintain an illumination level of 150 footcandles.

Lighting in the stock room and receiving areas is designed to provide an illumination level of 50 footcandles. Lighting fixtures in these areas are surface-mounted strips with exposed unshielded fluorescent tubes for economy.

The lighting layout for the stairways, as well as in all alteration rooms, is arranged to maintain a lighting level of 100 footcandles. All lighting fixtures in these areas are acrylic-shielded fluorescents—surface-mounted in some locations and recessed in others.

The show windows near the main store entrance are illuminated to a level of 500 footcandles by utilizing high-intensity shielded and adjustable spotlighting fixtures. Two or more different light sources in these areas would have provided more versatility for displays, but economy had to be considered.

All fitting rooms are provided with wall-mounted shielded fluorescent fixtures over the mirror in the dressing booths and a ceiling-mounted acrylic-shielded fluorescent fixture in the center of the fitting area. This arrangement provides an average illumination level of 100 footcandles, 150 footcandles on the mirror.

Exit lights have stenciled faces and cast-aluminum bodies, and use fluorescent lamps. They are also designed to serve as emergency downlights, and provide five footcandles of illumination at the door.

No unshielded fluorescent fixture is in any area which will be visited by the public.

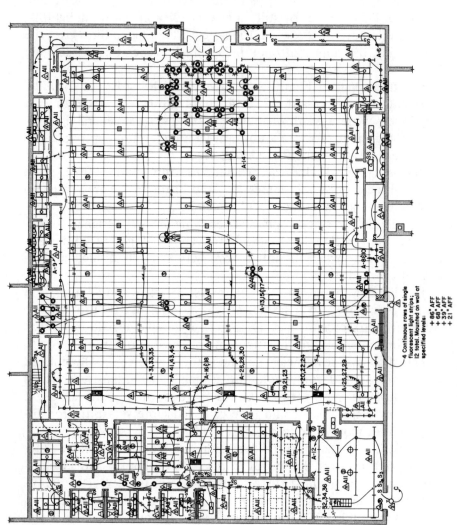

Fig. 5-7. Department store lighting layout utilizing several types of fluorescent and incandescent lighting fixtures.

All incandescent lamps are either inside-frosted or silver bowl, as required. The fluorescent lamps in the sales area, beauty salon, fitting rooms, toilets, and hall, as well as in storage rooms, are standard warm white for color quality. Cool-white fluorescent lamps are used in all offices, bulk-storage areas, alteration rooms, shipping and marking areas, and stairways.

The perimeter lighting shown in Figure 5–8 highlights the merchandise shelves around the perimeter of the store. Although all these lamps are bare tubes, the light sources are not readily visible to the public.

The remaining filament (incandescent) lighting in the sales areas consists of either recessed downlights or adjustable spots and are used for various merchandise displays as required by the store-fixture layout.

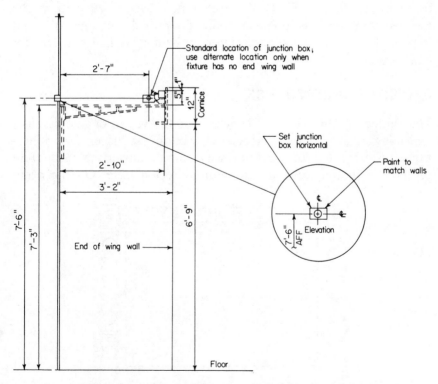

Fig. 5–8. Sectional view of shelf lighting for the department store in Fig. 5–7.

Dressing and powder rooms may use fluorescent lights for general illumination, but to flatter the complexion, incandescent lights—like the ones shown in Figure 5–9—should be installed around mirrors so that make-up can be applied.

Figure 5–10 shows a floor plan of a small office building. Twenty-nine 2' × 4' fluorescent lighting fixtures are the predominant sources of light for the entire building and are identified as Type One. Fluorescent fixtures are also used in the toilet and corridor.

Recessed incandescent lighting fixtures are used in a file storage area/lunch room and as perimeter lighting mounted in the soffit on three sides of the building. Wall bracket incandescent fixtures are used at each of the two doors.

The previous paragraphs have discussed several lighting projects where combinations of two or more different light sources were used simutaneously. While these examples barely touch upon the various combinations possible, they do provide an idea of what is possible so that any such design may be approached with greater confidence.

CHOICE OF LIGHT SOURCE

The choice of light source—filament, mercury vapor, or fluorescent—depends largely on appearance and economics. In certain applications, the large area of the fluorescent lamp is advantageous because of its low luminance and minimum reflected glare. On the other

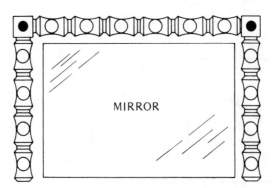

Fig. 5–9. Elevation view of theatrical make-up lighting around a mirror.

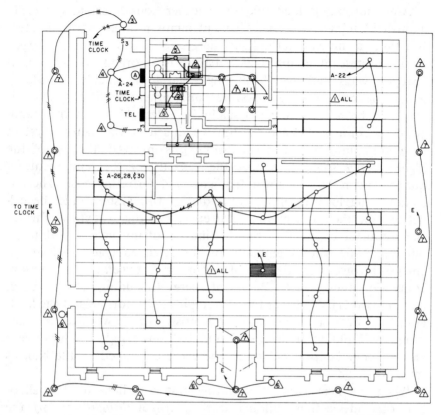

Fig. 5-10. Floor plan showing lighting layout of a small office building.

hand, where accurate control is desired, the smaller sources with their higher luminances are more effective.

The operating characteristics of fluorescent or mercury vapor lamps must be carefully considered if they will be installed in locations where they will be turned on and off at frequent intervals. or where they will be subjected to excessive fluctuations in supply voltage or to temperature extremes. In cases where existing wiring capacity limits wattage load, a fluorescent or mercury installation is often the only possible solution to the problem of providing higher illumination levels. Under some circumstances, light-source color and the creation of a pleasing effect may be a determining factor in choosing one or another type of lamp.

Air-conditioning load may be another consideration, especially at high illumination levels. Filament lamps produce approximately five times as much total radiant energy, for a given amount of light, as do fluorescent lamps. This radiation is absorbed in the form of heat by walls, ceilings, furnishings, and room occupants, which, depending on room temperatures and other conditions, may or may not be an advantage. Usually it is desirable from the standpoint of comfort to keep the heat produced by the lighting system to a minimum. Where air-conditioning is involved, the use of the higher-energy sources reduces the capacity of the equipment required, and results in lower first cost and operating cost. The air-conditioning load resulting from the lighting system must be calculated on the basis of the total energy of the system. A further analysis must be made of the distribution of this energy within the building, with primary emphasis on the occupied space. A thorough analysis involves a breakdown of this energy between (1) conduction-convection energy and (2) radiant energy (including light, infrared, and ultraviolet). Factors such as humidity, air motion, and the heat-absorbing or heat reflecting characteristics of luminaires and surrounding building materials should be considered. In fluorescent and mercury lamp installations, the watts consumed by the ballasts must be included.

When the heat from the lighting system will be used as all or part of cold weather building heating (*heat with light* system), the consideration of total energy distribution must, of course, include building heating. References on these matters can be found in the section on Light and Air Conditioning in the *IES Lighting Handbook* and in the *Guide of the American Society of Heating, Refrigeration and Air-Conditioning Engineers.*

Besides these special considerations, the choice of a light source is largely a matter of a cost analysis involving original cost of equipment and wiring, operating cost including power, maintenance, and lamp replacements, and other related items.

CHOICE OF EQUIPMENT

Proper candlepower distribution for the particular lighting application should be the first consideration in the selection of lighting equipment. Luminaires should be chosen for distribution characteristics suitable to the requirements of the given situation.

The efficiency of a luminaire is one measure of the quality of its material and design. Any control applied to the light output of a bare lamp results in some absorption of light. Ordinarily, the greater the degree of control attained, the greater the light loss. In many installations, the use of low-efficiency equipment is justifiable in order to achieve a desired effect. It is therefore impractical to compare the efficiencies of dissimilar types of equipment. However, luminaires which produce the same type of control can be compared on an efficiency basis, and those with higher efficiencies are preferred.

Electrical features of luminaires warrant careful consideration in the interest of trouble-free, efficient operation. Equipment built to conform to underwriters' specifications and that is certified by laboratory tests can usually be relied upon to provide the most satisfactory results.

Mechanical construction is important in all types of luminaires, but it requires special attention in those designed for the longer fluorescent light sources. The metal parts must be sufficiently strong to maintain the various elements in proper alignment and to safely support the comparatively heavy equipment. The accessibility of lamps and other electrical parts for service and cleaning is also an important consideration.

The appearance of the luminaire should be studied with respect to the architecture and decoration of the area in which it is to be used. The requirements will depend to some extent on whether the lighting equipment is functional, decorative, or both. In any event, the equipment should harmonize with the surroundings in architectural style, size, and decorative motif.

QUALITY OF ILLUMINATION

Comfortable seeing conditions in various areas can be obtained only if luminaire luminances are limited by adequately shielding the light source. The degree of brightness control required is dependent upon the source used, the size of the room, the illumination level, the reflectances and finish of room surfaces and furniture, and the nature of the visual task.

Figure 5–11 illustrates the direct and reflected glare zones as commonly defined.

Luminaires which have too high luminances in the direct glare zone produce direct glare. If luminances in the reflected glare zone are too high, there will be veiling reflections (loss of visibility) from specular components in the task surface, shiny pencil marks for example.

Luminaire luminances have been specified, measured, and reported as maximum luminance—the brightest square inch as seen from any viewing direction. However, recent investigations indicate that for the direct glare zone, average luminance (candlepower at any given angle divided by the projected luminous area of the luminaire at that angle) is a better criterion to use, provided the maximum luminance is not greater than about five times the average.

A general guide to acceptable luminance limits for fluorescent luminaires in schools or fairly large office areas is given in the accompanying Figure 5–12. If the average luminance of a luminaire at each of the angles in Figure 5–12 does not exceed the luminances in any single column, the luminance will meet the generally accepted limits for control of direct glare.

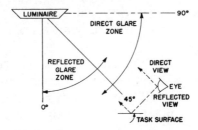

Fig. 5–11. Direct and reflected glare zones of a typical fixture.

Angle	Average Luminance (Footlamberts)								
85°	250	240	230	220	210	200	190	180	165
75°	250	250	250	250	250	250	250	250	250
65°	250	265	280	295	310	325	340	355	375
55°	250	285	315	350	385	415	450	480	535
45°	250	.310	365	420	480	540	600	660	750

Fig. 5–12.

A comfortable balance of perceived luminances in the office requires that the luminance ratios between areas of appreciable size from normal viewpoints be within the following:

1 to 1/3   Between task and adjacent surroundings.
1 to 1/10   Between task and more remote darker surfaces.
1 to 10   Between task and more remote lighter surfaces.
20 to 1   Between luminaires (or fenestration) and surroundings adjacent to them.
40 to 1   Anywhere within the normal field of view.

The above ratios should be considered as maximums; reductions will generally be favorable. In school rooms, the acceptable ratios are similar except that present research indicates that the 1 to 10 ratio should be reduced as the illumination level is increased above 50 footcandles.

LUMINAIRE LOCATION AND ORIENTATION

Large Offices

In very large offices the luminaire luminance is especially important because of the large number of luminaires that fall within the normal field of view. Furthermore, since there is often no predominant line of sight, the luminaires should be of acceptable luminance when viewed from any direction. With such equipment, the positioning of the luminaires is not critical as long as they are spaced to give

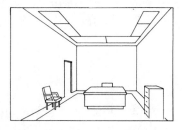 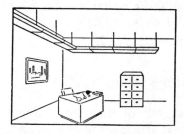

Fig. 5–13. Recessed and pendant-lighting fixtures arranged for top quality lighting in office spaces.

uniform distribution of light throughout the room. In large offices where desks are placed against the wall, additional luminaires should be provided near the wall to keep the illumination up to room average. Whenever there is a predominating line of sight, the luminaires should be oriented to take advantage of their lowest luminances and smallest luminous areas.

Classrooms and Classroom-Size Offices

In these rooms the predominant line of sight is generally more clearly defined than it is in large offices, and luminaires should always be positioned so that the smallest luminous area or the lowest luminance is presented to the line of sight.

Classrooms are generally provided with chalkboards along one or more walls. To increase the brightness of these relatively low-reflectance surfaces and at the same time improve the visibility of material presented on the board, supplementary lighting is sometimes desirable. If this supplementary illumination is controlled so that it is confined to the chalkboard area, the brightness difference between the chalkboard and the more highly reflecting adjacent wall will be reduced.

Small or Private Offices

Luminaires mounted in a U-, L- or rectangular-shaped pattern often provide the most efficiently utilized and the best quality lighting for rooms of this size. The luminaires should be positioned around the actual work areas in such a way that there is no reflected glare from desks or table tops. Fluorescent luminaires mounted at right angles to each other provide better diffusion than they do when mounted parallel.

Drafting Rooms

Quality is of the utmost importance in drafting rooms. This means special attention to the minimizing of direct glare, veiling reflections (reflected glare), and shadows along edges of T-squares and triangles or shadows from the draftsman's hands. Good solutions can be found by using indirect, semiindirect or other forms of overall ceiling lighting of carefully controlled luminances. The use of near-vertical drafting boards can reduce problems of shadows and reflections. Where the above luminaire systems are not feasible, shadows may be lessened by positioning luminaires or drafting tables to establish an angle of 15 to 20° between major straightedges and the long axes of luminaires.

Corridors, Halls, and Stairways

Although the illumination in these areas should not be spotty, the distribution need not be as uniform as that required for general lighting in rooms. For this reason it is permissible to exceed the usual maximum spacing-to-mounting-height ratio by as much as 50%. Good practice calls for any average illumination level not less than 20% of that in adjacent areas or 20 footcandles, whichever is greater.

Chapter 6

Lighting Calculations

This chapter is designed to give the reader a basic knowledge of the lighting calculations that are in current use throughout the industry. Several methods will be discussed, and the reader should be aware that each method has its applications and that none is suitable for all cases.

Lighting calculations really provide nothing more than reasonably accurate estimates which must be supplemented by the judgment and experience of the lighting designer. In most cases, there will be more than one solution for any lighting problem; some are dull and commonplace, whereas others show imagination and resourcefulness on the part of the designer. This chapter will help the designer to determine the amount of illumination required for any given area, but the other chapters in this book are necessary to obtain a lighting design with the highest visual comfort and performance consistent with the type of area to be illuminated and the budget provided by the architect or owners.

SQUARE FOOT METHOD FOR
DETERMINING ILLUMINATION LEVELS

The simplest method of designing a general lighting layout is by the watts or lumens per square foot method. This method is especially useful in areas where one type of illuminaire is used, and thus the mounting height of each is the same. This method also provides a very handy method for determining the number of lighting fixtures required and the size of lamps (wattage) to use in each for residential lighting applications.

When using this method, keep in mind that lighter wall and ceiling colors reflect more light and the darker colors absorb more light. The tables contained herein are based on rooms with light ceiling and wall colors; therefore, if the calculations are used for areas with dark-colored surfaces, the total lumens obtained in the calculations should be multiplied by a factor of at least 1.25 to ensure that the proper minimum amount of illumination will be provided in the final design and installation. These tables are also based on surface-mounted lighting fixtures. If the area to be lighted contains recessed fixtures, the total lumens obtained from the recessed fixtures should be multiplied by a factor of 0.60.

Table 6-1. Minimum recommended lumens per square foot for various residential areas.

Area	Lumens Required per Sq Ft
Living room	80
Kitchen	80
Dining room	45
Bathroom	65
Hallway	45
Laundry	70
Workshop (over workbench)	70
Bedroom	50

Multipurpose rooms, such as the family/recreation room, should have means of varying the illumination for different activities. This is accomplished either by controlling (switching) several groups of lights or with a dimmer control.

To begin a lighting calculation for a residential area, the designer must first obtain the room dimensions—either by scaling drawings or taking actual measurements. For example, a floor plan of a living room is shown in Figure 6-1. In scaling the drawing, assume that the area is 23 × 15 and equals 345 square feet. This figure is then multiplied by the required lumens per square foot, obtained from Table 6-1, to obtain the total lumens required:

$$345 \text{ (ft}^2) \times 80 \text{ (lumens required per ft}^2) = 27,600 \text{ lumens}$$

The next step is to refer to manufacturers' lamp data, such as those shown in Figure 6-2, to select lamps that will give the required

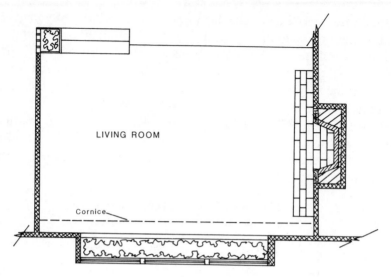

LIVING ROOM

Cornice

Fig. 6–1. Floor plan of a living room.

lumens. At the same time, the designer should refer to residential lighting fixture catalogs to get an idea of the types of fixtures to use in the area.

The lighting layout for the living room in question is shown in Figure 6–3. Here, four recessed "wall-wash" lighting fixtures are mounted in the ceiling in front of the fireplace to highlight the stone facing of the fireplace and chimney. The fixture catalog states that this type of lighting fixture will accept incandescent lamps up to 150 watts. The lamp data in Figure 6–2 indicate that a 150–watt I.F. (inside frosted) lamp has approximately 2880 lumens; thus, the four lamps used in this part of the living room give a total of 11,520 lumens. However, since the fixtures are recessed, the total lumen output must be multiplied by a factor of 0.60; this gives a total of only 6912 usable lumens. This means an additional 20,688 lumens will be required to reach the recommended values.

A drapery cornice is placed along the entire front wall at the windows. This cornice contains five 40–watt two-tube fluorescent fixtures installed behind the cornice. Each warm-white fluorescent lamp is rated at 2080 lumens, which gives a total of 20,800 lumens for the five fixtures. However, these fixtures are again not surface-mounted,

LAMP LUMEN OUTPUT TABLE

Incandescent

Watts	Bulb	Designation and finish	Approx. initial lumens
25	A-19	Inside Frosted	232
		Soft-White	222
40	A-19	Inside Frosted	450
		Soft-White	435
		Dawn Pink	340
50	A-19	Inside Frosted	680
60	A-19	Inside Frosted	855
		Soft-White	840
		Dawn Pink	650
75	A-19	Inside Frosted	1170
		Soft-White	1140
		Dawn Pink	870
		Sky Blue	450
100	A-19	Inside Frosted	1750
		Soft-White	1710
100	A-21	Dawn Pink	1200
		Sky Blue	610
150	A-21	Inside Frosted	2830
		Soft-White	2710
150	R-40	Soft-White	2300
200	A-23	Inside Frosted	3940
		Soft-White	3840

Clear spots and floodlights

Watts	Finish and beam type	Bulb designation	Approx. initial lumens
30	Spot	R-20	200
50	Spot	R-20	430
75	Spot or Flood	PAR-38	745
75	Spot or Flood	R-30	860
150	Spot or Flood	PAR-38	1730
150	Spot or Flood	R-40	1950

Colored spots and floodlights

Percent initial lumen output — colored sources as relates to corresponding clear floodlights.

Watts and bulb designation	Amber	Blue	Blue white	Green	Pink	Red	Yellow
50wR20	—	—	55	—	74	—	—
75wR30/ 150wR40	35	10	30	15	60	15	95
100wPAR38	57	5	39	17	52	7	77
150wPAR38 DICHRO SP/FL	52	6	—	18	—	27	78

NOTE: Flair Chandelight as well as colored light sources are generally for decorative lighting and would not be included in a total lumen count.

3-Way bulbs

30/70/100	A-21	Soft-White	275/1010/1285
50/100/150	A-23	Soft-White	560/1630/2190
		Dawn Pink (med. base)	435/1253/1688
50/100/150	R-40	Soft-White Indirect	560/1630/2190
50/200/250	PS-25	Soft-White	550/3560/4110
100/200/300	PS-25	Soft-White	1290/3440/4730
		Dawn Pink (mogul base)	968/2580/3548

Fluorescent

Deluxe warm- or cool-white fluorescent

Watts	Identification	Tube designation, thickness and length	Approx. initial lumens
14	WWX or CWX	T-12 (1½" × 15")	460
15	WWX or CWX	T-8 (1" × 18")	600
15	WWX or CWX	T-12 (1½" × 18")	505
20	WWX or CWX	T-12 (1½" × 24)	820
30	WWX or CWX	T-8 (1" × 36")	1520
30	WWX or CWX	T-12 (1½" × 36")	1480
40	WWX or CWX	T-12 (1½" × 48")	2080

Deluxe warm- or cool-white circline fluorescent

Watts	Identification	Tube designation, thickness and diameter	Approx. initial lumens
22	WWX or CWX	T-9 (1⅛" × 8¼")	745
32	WWX or CWX	T-10 (1¼" × 12")	1240
40	WWX or CWX	T-10 (1¼" × 16")	1760

NOTE: Deluxe white fluorescents render colors as they really are rather than distorting. Deluxe warm-white nearly duplicates the color of incandescent light while deluxe cool-white closely resembles daylight.

SOURCE: The General Electric Company.

Fig. 6–2. Table of manufacturer's lamp data.

60 WATTS

A-19	Medium											
	Medium	60A		120	.34	Inside Frosted (11)	120	CC-6	4⁷⁄₁₆	3⅛	1000	870
		60A	24PK PM	120	.34	Inside Frosted. 24-Pack PRICE MARKED	120	CC-6	4⁷⁄₁₆	3⅛	1000	870
		60A/TF	24PK	115-125	.76	Inside Frosted—TUFF-SKIN 24-Pack (44)	120	CC-6	4⁷⁄₁₆	....	1000	....
		60A		125	.37	Inside Frosted (11)	120	CC-6	4⁷⁄₁₆	3⅛	1000	870
		60A		130	.41	Inside Frosted (11)	120	CC-6	4⁷⁄₁₆	3⅛	1000	870
		60A/W	24PK PM	120	.37	Soft-White. 24-Pack PRICE MARKED (11)	120	CC-6	4⁷⁄₁₆	....	1000	855
		60A/WP	24PK PM	120	4/1.98	Soft-White PLUS—24-Pack PRICE MARKED (11)	120	CC-6	4⁷⁄₁₆	3⅛	1500	820
		60A/CL		120	.39	Clear (11)	120	CC-6	4⁷⁄₁₆	3⅛	1000	870
		60A/CL	24PK PM	120	.39	Clear. 24-Pack PRICE MARKED (11)	120	CC-6	4⁷⁄₁₆	3⅛	1000	870
		60A/CL		130	.47	Clear (11)	120	CC-6	4⁷⁄₁₆	3⅛	1000	870

75 WATTS

A-19	Medium											
	Medium	75A		120	.34	Inside Frosted (11)	120	CC-6	4⁷⁄₁₆	3⅛	750	1190
		75A	24PK PM	120	.34	Inside Frosted. 24-Pack PRICE MARKED (11)	120	CC-6	4⁷⁄₁₆	3⅛	750	1190
		75A		125	.37	Inside Frosted (11)	120	CC-6	4⁷⁄₁₆	3⅛	750	1190
		75A		130	.41	Inside Frosted (11)	120	CC-6	4⁷⁄₁₆	3⅛	750	1190
		75A/W	24PK PM	120	.37	Soft-White. 24-Pack PRICE MARKED (11)	120	CC-6	4⁷⁄₁₆	3⅛	750	1170
		75A/WP	24PK PM	120	4/1.98	Soft-White PLUS. 24-Pack PRICE MARKED (11)	120	CC-6	4⁷⁄₁₆	3⅛	1500	1075
		75A/CL		120	.39	Clear (11)	120	CC-6	4⁷⁄₁₆	3⅛	750	1190
		75A/CL		130	.47	Clear (11)	120	CC-6	4⁷⁄₁₆	3⅛	750	1190
	▲Medium	75A/99		120	.44	Inside Frosted—Extended Service (11)	120	CC-6	4⁷⁄₁₆	3⅛	2500	1000
		75A/99	24PK	120	.44	Inside Frosted—Extended Service. 24-Pack (11)	120	CC-6	4⁷⁄₁₆	3⅛	2500	1000
		75A/99		130	.53	Inside Frosted—Extended Service (11)	120	CC-6	4⁷⁄₁₆	3⅛	2500	1000

100 WATTS

A-19	Medium											
	Medium	100A		120	.34	Inside Frosted—Bonus Line (46)	120	CC-8	4⁷⁄₁₆	3⅛	750	1750
		100A	24PK PM	120	.34	Inside Frosted—Bonus Line. 24-Pack PRICE MARKED (46)	120	CC-8	4⁷⁄₁₆	3⅛	750	1750
		100A		125	.37	Inside Frosted—Bonus Line (46)	120	CC-8	4⁷⁄₁₆	3⅛	750	1750
		100A		130	.41	Inside Frosted—Bonus Line (46)	120	CC-8	4⁷⁄₁₆	3⅛	750	1750
		100A/W	24PK PM	120	.37	Soft-White—Bonus Line. 24-Pack PRICE MARKED (46)	120	CC-8	4⁷⁄₁₆		750	1710
		100A/WP	24PK PM	120	4/1.98	Soft-White PLUS. 24-Pack PRICE MARKED (11)	120	CC-8	4⁷⁄₁₆		1500	1585
		100A/CL		120	.39	Clear—Bonus Line (46)	120	CC-8	4⁷⁄₁₆	3⅛	750	1750
		100A/CL	24PK PM	120	.39	Clear—Bonus Line. 24-Pack PRICE MARKED (46)	120	CC-8	4⁷⁄₁₆	3⅛	750	1750
		100A/CL		130	.47	Clear—Bonus Line (46)	120	CC-8	4⁷⁄₁₆	3⅛	750	1750
	▲Medium	100A/99		120	.47	Inside Frosted—Extended Service (46)	120	CC-8	4⁷⁄₁₆	3⅛	2500	1490
		100A/99	24PK	120	.47	Inside Frosted—Extended Service. 24-Pack (46)	120	CC-8	4⁷⁄₁₆	3⅛	2500	1490
		100A/99		130	.57	Inside Frosted—Extended Service (46)	120	CC-8	4⁷⁄₁₆	3⅛	2500	1490
	▲Left-Hand Medium	100A/LHT		120	.41	Inside Frosted—Left-hand threaded base (11)	120	CC-8	4⁷⁄₁₆	3⅛	750	1750
		100A/LHT		130	.49	Inside Frosted—Left-hand threaded base (11)	120	CC-8	4⁷⁄₁₆	3⅛	750	1750

Fig. 6–2. Table of manufacturer's lamp data. (cont'd)

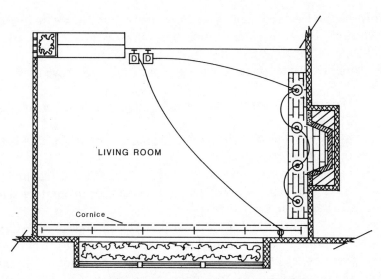

Fig. 6–3. Lighting layout for the living room in Fig. 6–1.

and therefore a factor of 0.60 will have to be used to obtain the actual lumens received.

$$20,800 \times 0.60 = 12,480 \text{ usable lumens}$$

This means that the room is still short [27,600 − (6912 + 12,480)] 8,208 lumens from the recommended amount determined earlier.

Although not shown on the floor plan in Figure 6–3, two three-way lamps (100, 200, and 300 watts) are used in table lamps on end tables located in the area. This gives an additional 9460 lumens in the area, for a total of 28,852 lumens—close enough to the total recommendations to be nearly perfect. As a final touch, dimmers are added to control the recessed fixtures at the fireplace and at the cornice. Since the two three-way lamps can be dimmed by switching to different wattages, the lighting levels in this area can be varied to suit the activities; low for a relaxed mood or bright for a gay party mood.

This method makes it possible to determine quickly and accurately the number and size of light sources needed to achieve the recommended lighting level in any area of the home. Of course, there are many different layouts that may be used for each area of the home, and the final decision will depend upon the owners and the designer.

This method merely tells you how many lumens are required for each area. Since there are numerous variables involved in selecting the types of lighting fixtures for a given application, no set rules are available. However, the following guidelines should prove useful.

1. Determine the total lumens required for a given area from Table 6-1.
2. Study residential lighting catalogs to see what types of lighting fixtures are available.
3. Prepare a master plan of the area. Then select a fixture or fixtures that will fit into the architectural or decorating scheme of the area to be lighted.
4. Read the manufacturer's description of the fixture to determine the number and size of lamps recommended for use in those fixtures selected. Then look at the data in Figure 6-2 to obtain the lumen output of the lamps in the fixture.

ZONAL-CAVITY METHOD OF LIGHTING CALCULATIONS

The Illuminating Engineering Society (IES) zonal-cavity method of lighting calculations is used to determine the average maintained-illumination level on the work plane in a given lighting installation and also to determine the number of lighting fixtures of a particular type) required in a given area to provide the desired or recommended illumination level.

The illumination calculation sheet shown in Figure 6-4 is recommended when the zonal-cavity method is used. The illustration on this form shows that a room or area is separated into three ratios: ceiling cavity ratio (CCR), room cavity ratio (RCR) and floor cavity ratio (FCR). The cavity ratios of the three areas are found as follows:

$$RCR = \frac{5hrc\,(L + W)}{L \times W}$$

$$CCR = \frac{5hcc\,(L + W)}{L \times W}$$

$$FCR = \frac{5hfc\,(L + W)}{L \times W}$$

ILLUMINATION CALCULATION SHEET

FOR USE WITH THE IES ZONAL CAVITY METHOD

GENERAL INFORMATION

PROJECT IDENTIFICATION: _____
(GIVE NAME OF AREA AND/OR BUILDING AND ROOM NUMBER)
AVERAGE MAINTAINED ILLUMINATION FOR DESIGN: _____FOOTCANDLES.

LUMINAIRE DATA:
MANUFACTURER: _____   CATALOG NUMBER: _____
LAMPS (TYPE & COLOR): _____   NUMBER PER LUMINAIRE: _____
TOTAL LUMENS PER LUMINAIRE: _____   MAINTENANCE FACTOR: _____

SELECTION OF COEFFICIENT OF UTILIZATION

STEP 1: FILL IN SKETCH AT RIGHT

STEP 2: DETERMINE CAVITY RATIOS BY THE FORMULA:

$$\frac{5 \times h \begin{bmatrix} CC \\ RC \\ FC \end{bmatrix} \times (L+W)}{L \times W}$$

ROOM CAVITY RATIO, RCR = _____

CEILING CAVITY RATIO, CCR = _____

FLOOR CAVITY RATIO, FCR = _____

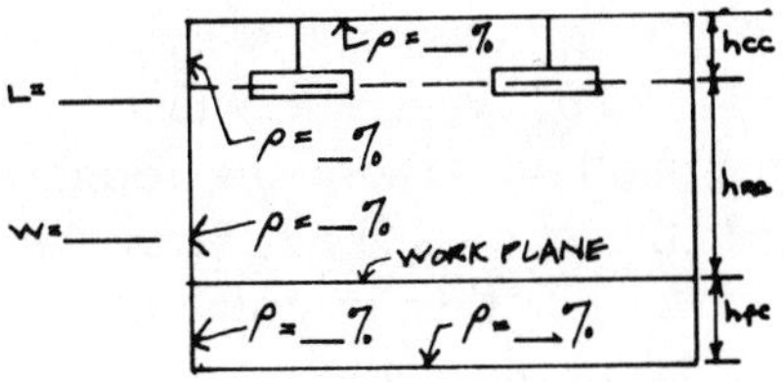

$L =$ _____ $W =$ _____

$\rho =$ __% $\rho =$ __% $\rho =$ __%   WORK PLANE $\rho =$ __% $\rho =$ __%

h_{CC} h_{RC} h_{FC}

STEP 3: OBTAIN EFFECTIVE CEILING CAVITY REFLECTANCE (ρ_{CC}). $\rho_{CC} =$ _____

STEP 4: OBTAIN EFFECTIVE FLOOR CAVITY REFLECTANCE (ρ_{FC}). $\rho_{FC} =$ _____

STEP 5: OBTAIN COEFFICIENT OF UTILIZATION (CU) FROM MANUFACTURER'S DATA.   CU = _____

CALCULATIONS

STEP 6:

AVERAGE MAINTAINED ILLUMINATION LEVEL

$$\text{FOOTCANDLES} = \frac{\text{(TOTAL LAMP LUMENS PER LUMINAIRE)} \times \text{(CU)} \times \text{MAINTENANCE FACTOR}}{\text{AREA PER LUMINAIRE}}$$

= _____

= _____ FOOTCANDLES ON WORK AREA

AREA PER LUMINAIRE: (THIS AREA DIVIDED BY THE LUMINAIRE LENGTH GIVES THE APPROXIMATE SPACING BETWEEN CONTINUOUS ROWS, OR IT MAY BE DIVIDED INTO THE TOTAL ROOM AREA TO DETERMINE THE NUMBER OF LUMINAIRES REQUIRED.)

$$\text{AREA PER LUMINAIRE} = \frac{\text{(TOTAL LAMP LUMENS PER LUMINAIRE)} \times \text{(CU)} \times \text{MAINTENANCE FACTOR}}{\text{FOOTCANDLES}}$$

= _____

= _____ SQUARE FEET.

CALCULATED BY: _____   DATE: _____

Fig. 6-4. Illumination calculation sheet.

where

hrc = height of room cavity (see drawing in Figure 6–4)

hcc = height of ceiling cavity (see drawing in Figure 6–4)

hfc = height of floor cavity (see drawing in Figure 6–4)

L = room length

W = room width

From these equations, we see that the cavity ratio for any area is found by multiplying the height of the cavity in question by five times the sum of the area's length and width and then dividing by the product of the area's length and width.

To begin a calculation for an area using the IES zonal-cavity method, record the room width and length, the ceiling height, and the mounting height of the lighting fixture above the floor, and fill in all other manufacturers' data shown in the form in Figure 6–4. Once all of the required information is inserted in the proper places on the form, calculate the three cavity ratios using the above equations. Insert the resulting data in the spaces provided for RCR, CCR, and FCR.

The next step is to select the effective ceiling cavity reflectance (PCC) from the chart in Figure 6–5 for the actual combination of ceiling and wall reflectances. Note that for surface-mounted or recessed lighting fixtures, CCR will equal 0, and the ceiling reflectance may be used as the effective cavity reflectance. Continue by selecting the effective floor cavity reflectance (PFC) for the combination on floor and wall reflectances, also found in the chart in Figure 6–5. Enter both these reflectance values in the illumination calculation sheet, such as the one in Figure 6–4.

The coefficient of utilization (CU) is determined by referring, for the lighting fixture under consideration, to a coefficient of utilization table such as the one in Figure 6–6. Coefficient of utilization tables are normally supplied in manufacturers' catalogs for each type of lighting fixture. If they are not shown in the catalog, ask the manufacturer to supply you with the required data. The CU is a measure of the total light flux received by a surface divided by the total

Effective Ceiling- or Floor-Cavity Reflectance for Various Reflectance Combinations

PER CENT CEILING OR FLOOR REFLECTANCE	90				80				70			50			30				10		
PER CENT WALL REFLECTANCE / Ceiling or Floor Cavity Ratio	90	70	50	30	80	70	50	30	70	50	30	70	50	30	65	50	30	10	50	30	10
0	90	90	90	90	80	80	80	80	70	70	70	50	50	50	30	30	30	30	10	10	10
0.1	90	89	88	87	79	79	78	78	69	69	68	59	49	48	30	30	29	29	10	10	10
0.2	89	88	86	85	79	78	77	76	68	67	66	49	48	47	30	29	29	28	10	10	9
0.3	89	87	85	83	78	77	75	74	68	66	64	49	47	46	30	29	28	27	10	10	9
0.4	88	86	83	81	78	76	74	72	67	65	63	48	46	45	30	29	27	26	11	10	9
0.5	88	85	81	78	77	75	73	70	66	64	61	48	46	44	29	28	27	25	11	10	9
0.6	88	84	80	76	77	75	71	68	65	62	59	47	45	43	29	28	26	25	11	10	9
0.7	88	83	78	74	76	74	70	66	65	61	58	47	44	42	29	28	26	24	11	10	8
0.8	87	82	77	73	75	73	69	65	64	60	56	47	43	41	29	27	25	23	11	10	8
0.9	87	81	76	71	75	72	68	63	63	59	55	46	43	40	29	27	25	22	11	9	8
1.0	86	80	74	69	74	71	66	61	63	58	53	46	42	39	29	27	24	22	11	9	8
1.1	86	79	73	67	74	71	65	60	62	57	52	46	41	38	29	26	24	21	11	9	8
1.2	86	78	72	65	73	70	64	58	61	56	50	45	41	37	29	26	23	20	12	9	7
1.3	85	78	70	64	73	69	63	57	61	55	49	45	40	36	29	26	23	20	12	9	7
1.4	85	77	69	62	72	68	62	55	60	54	48	45	40	35	28	26	22	19	12	9	7
1.5	85	76	68	61	72	68	61	54	59	53	47	44	39	34	28	25	22	18	12	9	7
1.6	85	75	66	59	71	67	60	53	59	52	45	44	39	33	28	25	21	18	12	9	7
1.7	84	74	65	58	71	66	59	52	58	51	44	44	38	32	28	25	21	17	12	9	6
1.8	84	73	64	56	70	65	58	50	57	50	43	43	37	32	28	25	21	17	12	9	6
1.9	84	73	63	55	70	65	57	49	57	49	42	43	37	31	28	25	20	16	12	9	6
2.0	83	72	62	53	69	64	56	48	56	48	41	43	37	30	28	24	20	16	12	9	6
2.1	83	71	61	52	69	63	55	47	56	47	40	43	36	29	28	24	20	16	13	9	6
2.2	83	70	60	51	68	63	54	45	55	46	39	42	36	29	28	24	19	15	13	9	6
2.3	83	69	59	50	68	62	53	44	54	46	38	42	35	28	28	24	19	15	13	9	6
2.4	82	68	58	48	67	61	52	43	54	45	37	42	35	27	27	23	19	14	13	9	6
2.5	82	68	57	47	67	61	51	42	53	44	36	41	34	27	27	23	18	14	13	9	6
2.6	82	67	56	46	66	60	50	41	53	43	35	41	34	26	27	23	18	13	13	9	5
2.7	82	66	55	45	66	60	49	40	52	43	34	41	33	26	27	23	18	13	13	9	5
2.8	81	66	54	44	66	59	48	39	52	42	33	41	33	25	27	23	17	12	13	9	5
2.9	81	65	53	43	65	58	48	38	51	41	33	40	33	25	27	22	17	12	13	8	5
3.0	81	64	52	42	65	58	47	38	51	40	32	40	32	24	27	22	17	12	13	8	5
3.1	80	64	51	41	64	57	46	37	50	40	31	40	32	24	27	22	17	12	13	8	5
3.2	80	63	50	40	64	57	45	36	50	39	30	40	31	23	27	22	16	11	13	8	5
3.3	80	62	49	39	64	56	44	35	49	39	30	39	31	23	27	22	16	11	13	8	5
3.4	80	62	48	38	63	56	44	34	49	38	29	39	31	.22	27	22	16	11	13	8	5
3.5	79	61	48	37	63	55	43	33	48	38	29	39	30	22	26	22	16	11	13	8	5
3.6	79	60	47	36	62	54	42	33	48	37	28	39	30	21	26	21	15	10	13	8	4
3.7	79	60	46	35	62	54	42	32	48	37	27	38	30	21	26	21	15	10	13	8	4
3.8	79	59	45	35	62	53	41	31	47	36	27	38	29	21	26	21	15	10	13	8	4
3.9	78	59	45	34	61	53	40	30	47	36	26	38	29	20	26	21	15	10	13	8	4
4.0	78	58	44	33	61	52	40	30	46	35	26	38	29	20	26	21	15	9	13	8	4
4.1	78	57	43	32	60	52	39	29	46	35	25	37	28	20	26	21	14	9	13	8	4
4.2	78	57	43	32	60	51	39	29	46	34	25	37	28	19	26	20	14	9	13	8	4
4.3	78	56	42	31	60	51	38	28	45	34	25	37	28	19	26	20	14	9	13	8	4
4.4	77	56	41	30	59	51	38	27	45	34	24	37	27	19	26	20	14	8	14	8	4
4.5	77	55	41	30	59	50	37	27	45	33	24	37	27	19	25	20	14	8	14	8	4
4.6	77	55	40	29	59	50	37	26	44	33	24	36	27	18	25	20	14	8	14	8	4
4.7	77	54	40	29	58	49	36	26	44	33	23	36	26	18	25	20	13	8	14	8	4
4.8	76	54	39	28	58	49	36	25	44	32	23	36	26	18	25	19	13	8	14	8	4
4.9	76	53	38	28	58	49	35	25	44	32	23	36	26	18	25	19	13	7	14	8	4
5.0	76	53	38	27	57	48	35	25	43	32	22	36	26	17	25	19	13	7	14	8	4

Courtesy Lightolier

Fig. 6–5. Table of ceiling, wall, and floor reflectance.

flux from the lamps illuminating it. When the CU has been determined, it should be entered in the illumination calculation sheet (Figure 6–4).

The maintenance factor (MF) is an estimation determined by several factors: the amount of dirt accumulation on the fixture prior to cleaning, the frequency of cleaning, the aging of the lamps, and the frequency of lamp replacement. This figure can vary, and it

Coefficients of Utilization
Zonal Cavity Method

Effective Floor Cavity Reflectance—20% ρfc										
Effective Ceiling Cavity Reflectance ρcc		80%			50%			10%		
% Wall Reflectance ρw		50%	30%	10%	50%	30%	10%	50%	30%	10%
NADIR C.P.-560 3100 Lumen Lamps	Room Cavity Ratios 1	.75	.70	.67	.67	.64	.61	.57	.55	.53
	2	.64	.57	.52	.57	.52	.48	.49	.46	.43
	3	.55	.48	.42	.49	.44	.39	.42	.39	.35
MAINTENANCE FACTORS Good .75 Med. .70 Poor .65	4	.49	.41	.36	.44	.38	.33	.38	.34	.30
	5	.42	.35	.29	.38	.32	.28	.33	.28	.25
	6	.38	.30	.25	.34	.28	.23	.29	.25	.21
Average Brightness in the 60°-90° zone from nadir shall not exceed 600 Foot-lamberts endwise or 1150 Footlamberis crosswise.	7	.34	.28	.22	.31	.25	.20	.27	.22	.19
	8	.30	.23	.18	.27	.21	.17	.24	.19	.16
	9	.27	.20	.16	.24	.19	.15	.21	.17	.14
	10	.25	.18	.14	.22	.17	.13	.20	.15	.12

Maximum Spacing to Mounting Height Ratio Above Work Plane is: 1.36

Fig. 6–6. Typical lighting fixture table giving coefficient of utilization data.

takes some experience to select the right one. However, Table 6–2 will serve as a guide, and the manufacturer will be able to help.

Table 6-2. Maintenance factor table.

Environment	MF
Very clean surroundings, such as hospitals	0.80
Clean surroundings, such as restaurants	0.75
Average surroundings, such as offices and schools	0.70
Below-average surroundings	0.65
Dirty surroundings	0.55

The manufacturer's catalog number is entered in the illumination sheet space marked "Lamp Type," the number of lamps used in the fixture is entered next, and then the number of the total watts per fixture is entered. The figure for lamp lumens can be found in lamp manufacturers' catalogs under the type of lamp used in the fixture. For the remaining calculations, refer to Step 6 in the form shown in Figure 6–4.

Lighting fixture locations depend on the general architectural style, size of bays, type of lighting fixtures under consideration, and similar factors. However, in order to provide even distribution of illumination for an area, the permissible maximum spacing recommendations should not be exceeded. These recommendation ratios are usually supplied by the fixture manufacturers in terms of maximum spacing to mounting height. In some cases the fixtures will have to be located closer together than these maximums in order to obtain the required illumination levels.

POINT-BY-POINT METHOD

The method for determining the average illumination of a given area was just described. However, it is sometimes desirable to know what the illumination level will be from one or more lighting fixtures upon a specified point within the area.

The point-by-point method accurately computes the level of illumination, in footcandles (fc), at any given point in a lighting installation. This is accomplished by summing up all the illumination contributions, except surface reflection to that point from every fixture individually. Since reflection from walls, ceilings, floors, etc., are not taken into consideration by this method, it is especially useful for calculations dealing with very large areas, outdoor lighting, and areas where the room surfaces are dark or dirty. With the aid of a candlepower distribution curve, we may calculate footcandle values for specific points as follows:

$$Fc = \frac{\text{candlepower} \times H}{d^3} \quad \text{or} \quad \frac{\text{candlepower} \times \cos^3 \theta}{H^2}$$

where

d = hypotenuse

H = height

Vertical Surfaces

In using the point-by-point method, a specific point is selected at which it is desired to know the illumination level, as, for example, point "P" in Figure 6–7. Once the seeing task or point has been determined, the illumination level at the point can be calculated.

$$Fc = \frac{\text{candlepower} \times R}{d^3} \quad \text{or} \quad \frac{\text{candlepower} \times \cos^3 \theta \times \sin \theta}{h^2}$$

The illumination at point "P" (in Figure 6–7), or at any point in the area, is due to light coming from all of the lighting fixtures. In

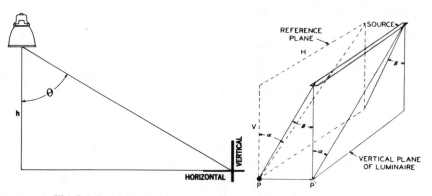

Fig. 6–7. Example showing use of point-by-point illumination method.

	Output Data		
HOLOPHANE COMPANY, INC. ENGINEERING CENTER NEWARK, OHIO Photometric Test Report	Zone Degrees	Lumens	% Total Lamp Lumens
	0–60	1975	52.0
	60–90	539	14.2
	90–180	786	20.7
	0–180	3300	86.9

Lamp C, IF
Lumens 3800
Watts 200
Volts 120
Amps.
Fil. CC–6
Bulb PS–25–IF
R.P.M. Lamp & Acc.–50
Test Distance 25 Feet
Test Cell No. G–6

Date May 20, 1957

Tested by J. R. Green

Certified by R. T. Smith
Manager of Photometric Dept.

Test of Holophane No. 02454

Test No. 18172

Fig. 6–8. Typical candlepower distribution curve.

θ°	sin θ	cos θ	cos² θ	cos³ θ	tan θ	θ°	sin θ	cos θ	cos² θ	cos³ θ	tan θ
0	0.0	1.000	1.000	1.000	0.0	46	0.719	0.695	0.483	0.335	1.035
1	.0175	1.000	1.000	1.000	.0174	47	.731	.682	.465	.317	1.072
2	.0349	0.999	0.999	0.998	.0349	48	.743	.669	.448	.300	1.110
3	.0523	.999	.997	.996	.0524	49	.755	.656	.430	.282	1.150
4	.0698	.998	.995	.993	.0699	50	.766	.643	.413	.266	1.191
5	.0872	.996	.992	.989	.0874	51	.777	.629	.396	.249	1.234
6	.105	.995	.989	.984	.1051	52	.788	.616	.379	.233	1.279
7	.122	.993	.985	.978	.1227	53	.799	.602	.362	.218	1.327
8	.139	.990	.981	.971	.1405	54	.809	.588	.345	.203	1.376
9	.156	.988	.976	.964	.1583	55	.819	.574	.329	.189	1.428
10	.174	.985	.970	.955	.1763	56	.829	.559	.313	.175	1.482
11	.191	.982	.964	.946	.1943	57	.839	.545	.297	.162	1.539
12	.208	.978	.957	.936	.2125	58	.848	.530	.281	.149	1.600
13	.225	.974	.949	.925	.2308	59	.857	.515	.265	.137	1.664
14	.242	.970	.941	.913	.2493	60	.866	.500	.250	.125	1.732
15	.259	.966	.933	.901	.2679	61	.875	.485	.235	.114	1.804
16	.276	.961	.924	.888	.2867	62	.883	.470	.220	.103	1.880
17	.292	.956	.915	.875	.3057	63	.891	.454	.206	.0936	1.962
18	.309	.951	.905	.860	.3249	64	.899	.438	.192	.0842	2.050
19	.326	.946	.894	.845	.3443	65	.906	.423	.179	.0755	2.144
20	.342	.940	.883	.830	.3639	66	.914	.407	.165	.0673	2.246
21	.358	.934	.872	.814	.3838	67	.921	.391	.153	.0597	2.355
22	.375	.927	.860	.797	.4040	68	.927	.375	.140	.0526	2.475
23	.391	.921	.847	.780	.4244	69	.934	.358	.128	.0460	2.605
24	.407	.914	.835	.762	.4452	70	.940	.342	.117	.0400	2.747
25	.423	.906	.821	.744	.4663	71	.946	.326	.106	.0347	2.904
26	.438	.899	.808	.726	.4877	72	.951	.309	.0955	.0295	3.077
27	.454	.891	.794	.707	.5095	73	.956	.292	.0855	.0250	3.270
28	.470	.883	.780	.688	.5317	74	.961	.276	.0762	.0211	3.487
29	.485	.875	.765	.669	.5543	75	.966	.259	.0670	.0173	3.732
30	.500	.866	.750	.650	.5773	76	.970	.242	.0585	.0142	4.010
31	.515	.857	.735	.630	.6008	77	.974	.225	.0506	.0114	4.331
32	.530	.848	.719	.610	.6248	78	.978	.208	.0432	.0090	4.704
33	.545	.839	.703	.590	.6494	79	.982	.191	.0364	.0070	5.144
34	.559	.829	.687	.570	.6745	80	.985	.174	.0302	.0052	5.671
35	.574	.819	.671	.550	.7002	81	.988	.156	.0245	.0038	6.313
36	.588	.809	.655	.530	.7265	82	.990	.139	.0194	.0027	7.115
37	.602	.799	.638	.509	.7535	83	.993	.122	.0149	.0018	8.144
38	.616	.788	.621	.489	.7812	84	.995	.105	.0109	.0011	9.514
39	.629	.777	.604	.469	.8097	85	.996	.0872	.0076	.0007	11.430
40	.643	.766	.587	.450	.8391	86	.9976	.0698	.0048	.0003	14.300
41	.656	.755	.570	.430	.8692	87	.9986	.0523	.0027	.0001	19.080
42	.669	.743	.552	.410	.9004	88	.9993	.0349	.0012	.0000	28.630
43	.682	.731	.535	.391	.9325	89	.9998	.0175	.0003	.0000	57.280
44	.695	.719	.517	.372	.9656	90	1.0000	0.0000	.0000	.0000	Infinite
45	.707	.707	.500	.354	1.0000						

Fig. 6–9. Table of trigonometric functions.

this case, the calculations must be repeated to determine the amount of light that each fixture contributes to the point; the total amount is the sum of all the contributing values.

Before attempting any actual calculations using the point-by-point method, a knowledge of candlepower distribution curves and a review of trigonometric functions is necessary.

A candlepower distribution curve or graph consists of lines plotted on a polar diagram which show graphically the distribution of the light flux in some given plane around the actual light source. It also shows the apparent candlepower intensities in various directions about the light source. Figure 6–8 illustrates a typical candlepower distribution curve.

A table of trigonometric functions (Figure 6–9) will be helpful in determining the degrees of the angle from the light source to the point in question. This is necessary to pick off the candlepower from the photometric distribution curve and also to use in the equations.

OUTDOOR LIGHTING

Illumination data for outdoor lighting fixtures are usually shown in the form of isofootcandle graphs as shown in Figure 6–10. These are regarded as the most useful form of data since they are actual representations of the lighting pattern and intensity at grace level on a horizontal plane. The curves on the graph are points of equal illumination (in lumens per square foot or footcandles), connected by a continuous line and are known as *isofootcandle* (IFC) or *isolux* lines.

Two types of isofootcandle graphs commonly used to express footcandle levels for outdoor lighting units are shown in Figures 6–11 and 6–12. Type I (Figure 6–11) is based on a fixed mounting height where the grid lines of the graph indicate actual distance in feet from the lighting unit. Type 2 (Figure 6–12) is computed for a

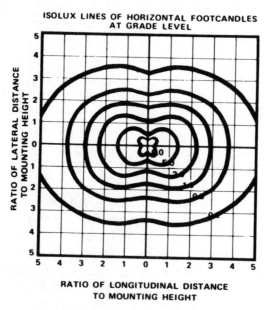

Fig. 6–10. Typical isofootcandle graph.

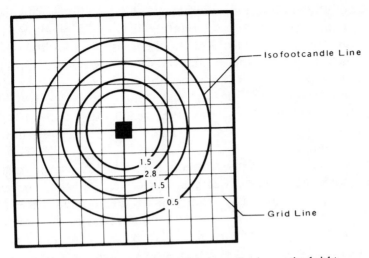

Fig. 6-11. Isofootcandle graph based on a fixed mounting height.

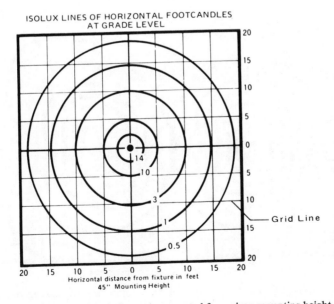

Fig. 6-12. Isofoot candle graph computed for a given mounting height.

given mounting height; however, the grid lines are indicated as ratios of the actual distance to the mounting height. The graph in Figure 6-12, for example, is calculated on the basis of a mounting height of 16 feet. To obtain the distance at which any of the isolux lines occurs, simply multiply the 16 feet by the corresponding grid-line ratio number. For example, at what distance does the IFC occur along the longitudinal distance from the lighting unit? The IFC isogrid line (1) is 16 feet, since 16 feet $\times$ 1 = 16 feet—the distance from the lighting unit.

The distance ratios allow correction factors (CF) to be used for other mounting heights. Correction factors for other mounting heights can be determined by dividing the square of the given mounting height by the square of the desired mounting height. For example, for a given mounting height of 16 feet (16 $\times$ 16 = 256), and a desired mounting height of 12 feet (12 $\times$ 12 = 144), then

$$CF = \frac{256}{144} = 1.77$$

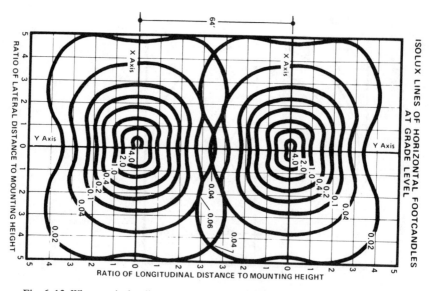

Fig. 6-13. Wherever isolux lines overlap, the two footcandle values are added together.

1.77 then becomes the correction factor to be applied to the foot-candle level on the isofootcandle graph for a 12-foot mounting height.

The Panorama isofootcandle graphs are based on a single lighting unit. They become extremely useful in determining exact lighting levels at any specific point and for determining quickly required spacing in order to attain desired footcandle levels. These graphs can be quickly transferred to actual overlays of plot plans or layouts and light levels noted in Figure 6-13. Wherever isolux lines overlap, the two footcandle values are added together.

It is difficult to establish ideal lighting levels for outdoor spaces since much depends on the lighting in surrounding areas and the focal points available as reference. The following guidelines can be considered minimums for safety and emphasis in a dark ambient.

Outdoor Space	Footcandles
General lighting	0.5
Paths, walkways, steps	1
Backgrounds—fences, walks, trees, etc.	2
Flower beds, gardens	5
Trees, shrubbery—when emphasized	5
Focal points—large	10
Focal points—small	20
Parking areas	1-2
Pedestrial building entrances	2

Chapter 7

Practical Lighting Applications

One of the best methods of learning practical lighting design is to study existing drawings of actual lighting installations. Unfortunately, printed working drawings of lighting systems are rare. Therefore, the basic purpose of this chapter is to remedy this situation by giving the reader a means of seeing and analyzing actual working drawings of lighting systems used in residential, commercial, institutional, and industrial structures.

RESIDENTIAL LIGHTING

The lighting layout and choice of lighting fixtures are two of the most important features of both interior and exterior decorating. They should be considered as important as the heating and cooling system, furniture placement, and the like, since properly designed lighting is one of the greatest comforts and conveniences that a homeowner can enjoy.

Kitchen Lighting

The lighting layout for the kitchen must always receive careful attention since this is the area most often used by the housewife.

The ideal general lighting system for a residential kitchen is shown in Figure 7-1. This plan shows bare fluorescent strips, with dimming control, installed 2 feet on centers above diffuser ceiling panels. This arrangement provides a "skylight" effect and is known as a *luminous ceiling*.

The fluorescent lamps used in the lighting layout in Figure 7-1 are

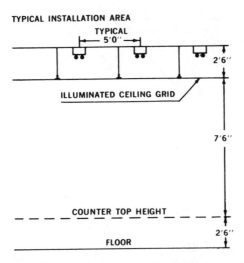

TYPICAL INSTALLATION AREA

TYPICAL ← 5'0" →

2'6"

ILLUMINATED CEILING GRID

7'6"

COUNTER TOP HEIGHT

2'6"

FLOOR

Fig. 7–1. The ideal general lighting system for a residential kitchen is a luminous ceiling.

Deluxe cool-white because they contain more red than they contain standard cool-white lamps—this emphasizes skin tones and is more flattering to the appearance of people. This type of lamp also gives a good appearance to lean meat, keeps fats white, and emphasizes the fresh, crisp appearance of green vegetables.

Another kitchen lighting plan is shown in Figure 7–2. Here, two surface-mounted ceiling fixtures with opal glass diffusers are used for general illumination; each fixture contains two 60–watt incandescent lamps. This light source accents and enriches the wood tones of the wall cabinets.

The fluorescent fixtures are located under the wall cabinets and behind a shielding board as shown in Figure 7–3. Warm-white fluorescent lamps are used as the best color for lighting the countertops. This shadow-free light not only accents the colorful countertops, but also makes working at the counter much more efficient and pleasant.

The two 75–watt R–30 floodlights installed over the kitchen sink (about 15 inches on center) offer excellent light for work at the sink.

The light for the electric range is provided in the ventilating hood mounted on the wall above the range. These self-contained lights consist of two 60–watt lamps and are switched on the hood itself.

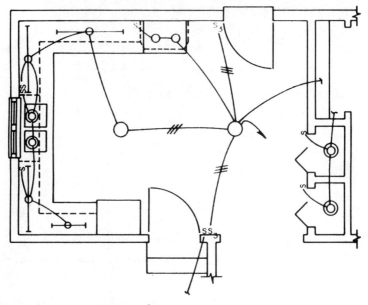

Fig. 7–2. Kitchen lighting plan utilizing both incandescent and fluorescent light sources.

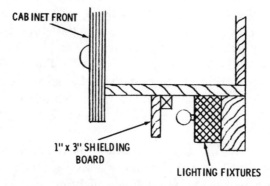

CABINET FRONT

1" x 3" SHIELDING BOARD

LIGHTING FIXTURES

Fig. 7–3. Detail of fluorescent fixtures located under the wall cabinets in Fig. 7–2.

Dining Areas

In homes with separate dining rooms, a chandelier mounted directly above the dining table and controlled by a dimmer switch becomes the centerpiece of the room while providing general illumination. The dimmer, of course, adds versatility since it can set the mood of the activity: low brilliance (candlelight effect) for formal dining or bright for an evening of cards. When chandeliers with exposed lamps are used, the dimmer control is essential to avoid an uncomfortable glare from the lamps. The size of the chandelier is also very important; it should be sized in proportion to the size of the dining area.

Good planning in the dining area calls for supplementary lighting at the buffet and sideboard areas. In a traditional decor, wall bracket fixtures that match the chandelier may be used. For a contemporary design, recessed accent light may be used in the ceiling. Additional supplementary lighting—for traditional or modern—may consist of concealed fluorescent lighting in valances or cornices.

LIVING ROOM

The living room is where guests are entertained and where the family gathers to relax or engage in conversation. The living room lighting should emphasize any special architectural features such as fire-places, bookcases, and so forth. This also holds true for special room accents, such as draperied walls, planters, and paintings.

Dramatizing fireplaces with accent or wall-wash lighting fixtures brings out the texture of the bricks, adds to the overall room light level, and eliminates bright spots that cause subconscious irritation over a period of time. Recessed lighting fixtures using from 75– to 150–watt lamps are excellent for this application.

A row of recessed downlights or cornice or valance lighting all add life to draperies, paneled walls, and the like. They also supplement the general room-lighting level with glare-free light.

The lighting fixtures used for living room accent lighting should be spaced approximately 2.5 to 3 feet apart and 8 to 10 inches from the wall (in case of wall-wash or bookcase lighting) and directly over such items as planters. Valances are nearly always used at windows or above draperied walls. They provide up-light, which reflects off the ceiling for general room lighting, and down-light for drapery accent. Cornices, on the other hand, direct all of their light downward to give dramatic interest to wall coverings and draperies. They are also good for low-ceiling rooms.

Pull-down fixtures or table lamps are used for reading areas. While pull-down fixtures are more dramatic than table lamps, the furniture placement must be known prior to locating the pull-down fixtures. Then there is the disadvantage of not being able to move the furniture once the lights are installed.

As a final touch to living room lighting, dimmers should be installed to vary the lighting levels exactly to the living room activities: low for a relaxed mood, bright for a happy party mood.

A floor plan of a living room lighting arrangement is shown in Figure 6–2, and an explanation of how the designer arrived at this layout is described in the text.

Bedroom Lighting

The majority of people spend at least a third of their lives in their bedroom. Still, the bedroom is often overlooked in terms of lighting as most homeowners prefer to concentrate their efforts and money on areas that will be seen more by visitors. However, proper lighting is very important in the bedroom for such activities as dressing, grooming, studying, reading, and for a relaxing environment in general.

Basically, bedroom lighting should be both decorative and functional with flexibility of control to create the desired lighting environment. For example, both reading and sewing (two common activites occuring in the bedroom) require good general illumination combined with supplementary light directed onto the page or fabric. Other activities, however, like casual conversation or watching television, require only general nonglaring room illumination, preferably controlled by a dimmer switch/control.

A typical master bedroom of a small residence is shown in Figure 7–4. Cornice lighting is used to highlight the colorfully draped wall and also to create an illusion of greater depth in this small bedroom. The wall-to-wall cornice board also lowers the apparent ceiling height in the room, which makes the room seem wider.

Two wall-mounted "swing-away" lamps on each side of the bed furnish reading light, while matched vanity lamps (not shown) provide light for grooming.

A single recessed lighting fixture in the closet provides adequate illumination for selecting clothes and identifying articles on the shelves. The light is controlled by a door switch which turns the light on when the door is opened and turns it out when the door is shut.

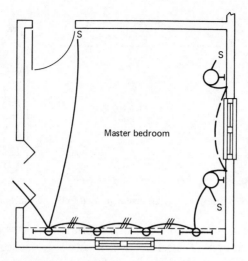

Fig. 7-4. Floor plan of a master bedroom.

Bathroom Lighting

Lighting performs a wide variety of tasks in the bathroom of the modern residence. Good light is essential for good grooming and hygiene practices.

The lavatory-vanity in the bath in Figure 7-5 is lighted to remove

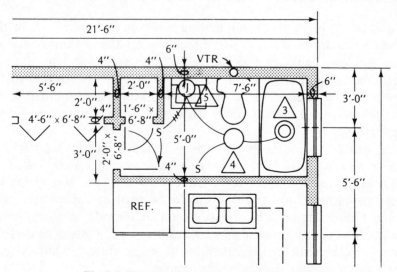

Fig. 7-5. Floor plan of a bathroom lighting layout.

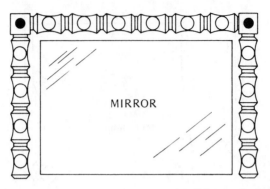

Fig. 7–6. Theatrical lighting arrangement used to light a vanity bath mirror.

all shadows from faces and from under chins for shaving. A theatrical lighting arrangement (Figure 7–6) is used to accomplish this. A moisture-proof, recessed fixture is also used over the tub for safety and health reasons, and a ceiling fixture with a sunlamp is used directly outside of the tub area for drying purposes and to aid in tanning the skin.

Larger bathrooms may require other ceiling-mounted fixtures, but generally, the layout just described is adequate for average bathrooms.

Workshop, Basement, and Utility Room Lighting

An example of utility room lighting is shown in Figure 7–7. In this plan, a laundry sink is installed into a counter and in front of an outside window, flanked on each side by cabinets. A two-lamp fluorescent fixture is mounted against the ceiling and directly above the sink; shallow under-cabinet fluorescent fixtures are mounted under the cabinets on each side of the sink to provide illumination on the countertops.

Lighting for ironing is best when a shadow-casting light is used above and in front of the operator, as shown in Figure 7–8. With this arrangement, the shadows fall toward the operator, giving the best visibility. These fixtures should be used in conjunction with general illumination which may be either incandescent or fluorescent. However, if fluorescent fixtures are used, remember that the lamps and ballasts are very sensitive to temperature and humidity. A vaporproof lens is therefore recommended.

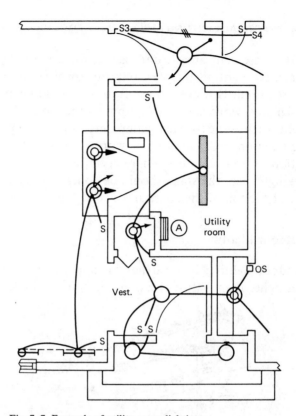

Fig. 7-7. Example of utility room lighting.

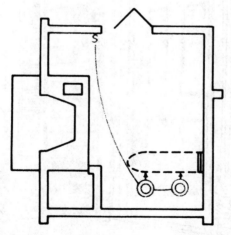

Fig. 7-8. Lighting for ironing is best when a shadow casting light is used above and in front of the operator.

If a basement area is unfinished, there naturally is no need to use expensive lighting fixtures; only inexpensive porcelain lamp holders are required. However, these fixtures should be located to illuminate designated work areas or equipment locations. All mechanical equipment, such as the furnace, pumps, etc., should be properly illuminated for maintenance. Laundry or work areas should have general illumination as well as areas where specific tasks are performed. At least one light near the stairs should be controlled by two 3-way switches, one at the top of the stairs and one at the bottom.

Outdoor Lighting

Outdoor lighting is a partner in modern living. It welcomes guests and lights their paths, creating a hospitable look. As a safety factor,

Fig. 7-9. A pair of outdoor wall bracket fixtures—one on each side of the entrance door—is basic for residential applications.

it protects the home from prowlers and reduces the incidence of outdoor accidents.

A pair of outdoor wall brackets, such as those shown at the front entrance on the floor plan in Figure 7–9, is basic. If a long walk is necessary, a decorative yet practical post lighting fixture should be included as well as low-level mushroom-type lighting fixtures.

The carport in the drawing in Figure 7–9 is a separate lighting area, and, as shown in the floor plan, an all-purpose lighting fixture centered in the ceiling is adequate to light the way to the back door.

COMMERCIAL LIGHTING

The floor plan of a branch bank in Figure 7–10 illustrates an application of lighting in a commercial building. Note that the general lighting is provided by recessed, 2' × 4' fluorescent troffer fixtures to provide approximately 100 footcandles of illumination. These

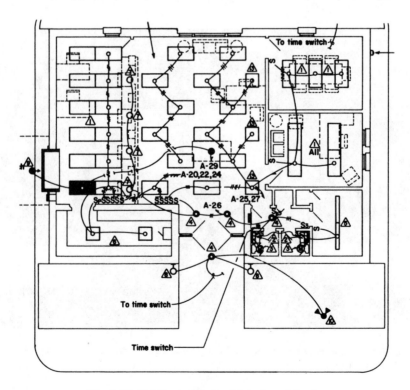

Fig. 7–10. Lighting arrangement for a branch bank.

fixtures are doubled over desks in office areas to provide approximately 200 footcandles of illumination.

The chandelier (Figure 7-11) is indicated by the solid circle on the floor plan and provides a decorative fixture during office hours and serves as a night light during closing periods.

The pendant cylinders over each teller area (Figure 7-12) are used as decorative fixtures as well as supplementary lighting—to increase the footcandle level to 150 footcandles—for teller functions.

Recessed down-lights are used in the vestibule to provide adequate lighting where the ambient temperature might be too low during cold weather to allow fluorescent fixtures to start properly.

The outside wall bracket fixtures shown in Figure 7-13 contain 100-watt incandescent lamps inside a frosted chimney to provide a colonial feeling that blends with the Williamsburg style of the building.

Fig. 7-11. The chandelier not only acts as a decorative fixture but also serves as a night light during closing periods.

Fig. 7–12. These pendant cylinders are used as decorative fixtures as well as supplementary lighting.

Nursing Home Laundry Building

Figure 7–14 is the floor plan of a laundry building constructed to handle the in-house laundry for a nursing home. Since the building is of a utility class and a limited budget was provided for its construction, a very simple, low-cost lighting layout was designed.

Bare-lamp, 4–foot, surface-mounted lighting fixtures are used in the clean linen area and in the corridor. Each fixture contains two 40–watt cool-white fluorescent lamps, and approximately 25 footcandles are provided in each area.

The office has two 18" × 4' fluorescent fixtures with acrylic prismatic diffusers which give the area over 150 footcandles of illumination.

Fig. 7-13. Outside wall bracket fixtures—each containing 100-watt incandescent lamps—provide a colonial feeling to blend with the Williamsburg style of the building.

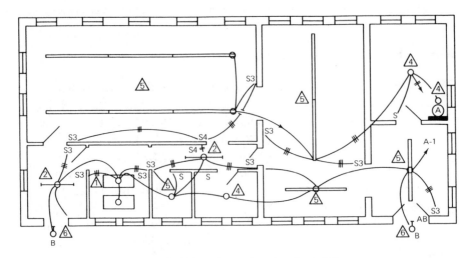

Fig. 7-14. Lighting layout for a laundry building.

Due to the fact that moisture is ever-present in the remaining areas of the laundry, enclosed and gasketed 8–foot fluorescent fixtures are used. Each of these fixtures contains one 8–foot, 150–watt fluorescent lamp and an 800–mA ballast. The acrylic clear prismatic lens on these fixtures provides for excellent light control; the prisms assure good brightness and hide lamp image. The continous one-piece vinyl gasketing has no seams and is therefore dirt-, dust-, bug-, and watertight.

INDUSTRIAL LIGHTING

Most industrial lighting applications are not color-critical, and all the HID light sources are usually satisfactory. The following suggestions for choosing the proper industrial light sources were furnished by General Electric.

1. Use Lucalox (high-pressure sodium) lamps where minimum cost of light is desired.
2. Use Multi-Vapor (tandem fixtures) where low-cost lighting and a cooler-appearing environment are desired.
3. Use semireflector deluxe white lamps in practically all mercury lamp applications. Some incandescent or fluorescent lighting fixtures should be added for standby lighting in case of a power

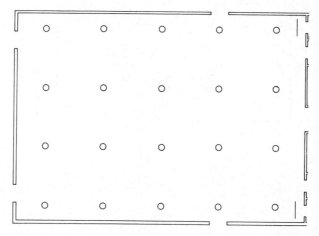

Fig. 7–15. Lighting system utilizing 400-watt mercury fixtures to produce an average of 100 footcandles of illumination.

interruption. Some HID lighting fixtures can be purchased with optional built-in quartz lamps connected to the same circuit which can be used for standby lighting.

4. Use silver-reflector mercury lamps in combination with silver-reflector filament lamps in areas with severe dir conditions.

The lighting system illustrated in Figure 7–15 consists of 400–watt mercury fixtures mounted 10' X 10' on centers and produces approximately 100 footcandles of illumination.

Supermarket Lighting

An application of HID lighting is shown in Figure 7–16. The required number of fixtures to produce the desired illumination level is calculated by using the zonal cavity method. Recessed HID lighting fixtures are used and are spaced 6 feet on center. The result of this design gives the ceiling a more spacious, clean, and nondistracting look. Hot spots and glare are kept to a minimum, while the acrylic refractors provide even illumination throughout the store area. Since the HID lamps provide more lumens per watt than incandescent or fluorescent fixtures, much energy is saved in both illumination and air-conditioning use.

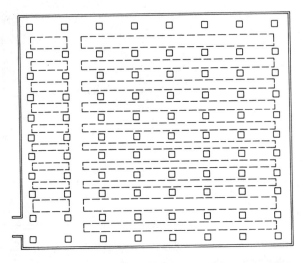

Fig. 7–16. Application of HID lighting used in supermarkets.

Chapter 8

Lighting Details

Although electrical designers usually describe a building's lighting system in working drawings consisting of floor plans, elevations, sections, and written specifications, certain construction conditions cannot be adequately shown in the scale in which these drawings are usually made. Therefore, larger-scaled drawings must be made of such items or areas to ensure the necessary information for proper construction. These are termed *special* or *large-scale* electrical detail drawings and are found in nearly every set of working drawings.

This chapter provides practical lighting details taken from actual working drawings and manufacturers' literature. Many of them have been used on a variety of projects for the past decade. All of the details, therefore, have been tried and proven to be useful to lighting designers and enable electrical contractors to bid and install the systems with the information furnished on the drawings from the information furnished by the lighting designer.

INSTALLATION DETAILS FOR DAY-BRITE MERCURY FIXTURES

Figure 8-1 shows mounting details for both round and square mercury fixtures. Although these details describe fixtures manufactured by Day-Brite, they will also apply to similar fixtures manufactured by others.

DAY-BRITE HANGING ACCESSORIES

The drawings in Figure 8-2 illustrate several types of hanging accessories available from Day-Brite. The captions under each describe their use.

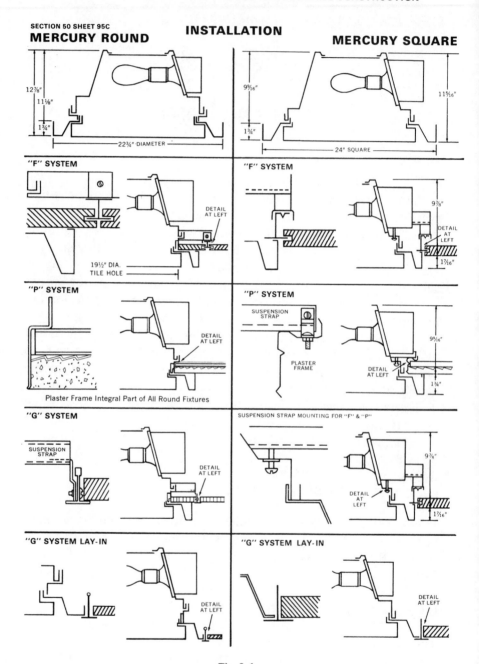

Fig. 8–1.

SURFACE CIRCULAR FIXTURES

Incandescent surface circular fixtures are available from The Kirlin Company in 100- through 500-watt capacity. The details in Figure 8-3 show some applications for these fixtures.

SURFACE SQUARE FIXTURES

The details in Figure 8-4 show various ways of mounting surface square incandescent fixtures.

INSTALLATION INSTRUCTIONS
FOR RECESSED FIXTURES

The drawings in Figure 8-5 give installation instructions for several types of recessed lighting fixtures, including the National Electric Code (NEC) requirements.

RECESSED SQUARE FIXTURES

The drawings in Figure 8-6 show mounting methods for square recessed fixtures on several types of hangers.

MISCELLANEOUS MOUNTING INSTRUCTIONS

The details in Figures 8-7a and 8-7b give several types of mounting situations along with NEC requirements.

DAY-BRITE HANGING ACCESSORIES

SECTION 30 SHEET 95G

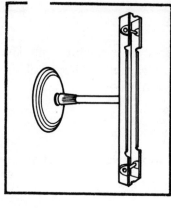

STEM-LINE SINGLE STEM HANGERS—8-inch SINGLE STEM HANGERS R-4158; 24-inch SINGLE STEM HANGERS R-4154; for 8-foot Units and Continuous MARKSMAN II Fixtures.

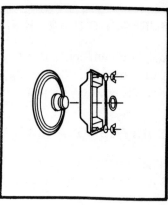

CEILING CANOPY HANGER R-3392 for use in place STEM HANGERS for CLOSE-TO-CEILING installation.

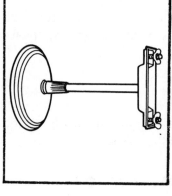

STEM-LINE SINGLE STEM HANGERS — 8-inch HANGERS R-4108; 24-inch HANGERS R-4124; for 8-ft. Units and Continuous Installations of LUVEX and other Commercial Fixtures (EXCEPT MARKSMAN II).

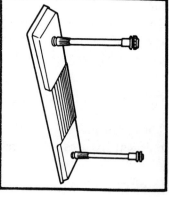

STEM-LINE TWIN-STEM HANGERS—8-inch TWIN-STEM HANGERS R-4208; 24-inch TWIN-STEM HANGERS R-4224; for 4-ft. Single Unit installations. PAT. NO. D-197,186

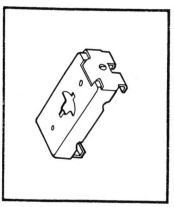

SLIDING CLAMP HANGER 3426 for use with LUVEX. Positions at any location along length of channel. Replaces bottom canopy on Nos. R-4108 or R-4124.

INDUSTRIAL TYPE BOTTOM SLIDE CLAMP HANGER 3448 for LUVEX & LITE STRIP. Replaces bottom canopy on Nos. R-7108 or R-7124.

SURFACE MOUNTING HANGER 3376 for "GRID-TEE" supported ceiling. All "TEES" 1-inch maximum width.

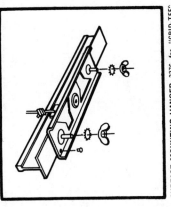

SURFACE MOUNTING HANGER R-3351 to provide spacing for Low-Density ceilings.

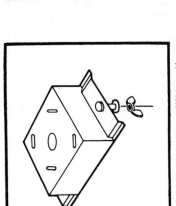

SLIDING CLAMP HANGER 3441 for use with MARKSMAN, HOLIDAY II, CHAN-L-ITE, and LITEWAY. Replaces bottom canopy on Nos. R-4108 or R-4124.

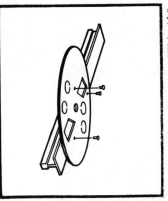

SURFACE MOUNTING HANGER 3378 for 1½" channel.

SUSPENSION MOUNTING HANGER R-3377-A and Collar for exposed grid supported ceilings.

Fig. 8-2.

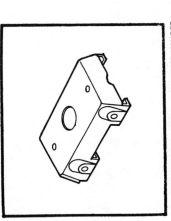

INDUSTRIAL TYPE BOTTOM SLIDE CLAMP HANGER 3471 for MARKSMAN, HOLIDAY II, CHAN-L-ITE, and LITEWAY. Replaces bottom canopy on Nos. R-7108 or R-7124.

157

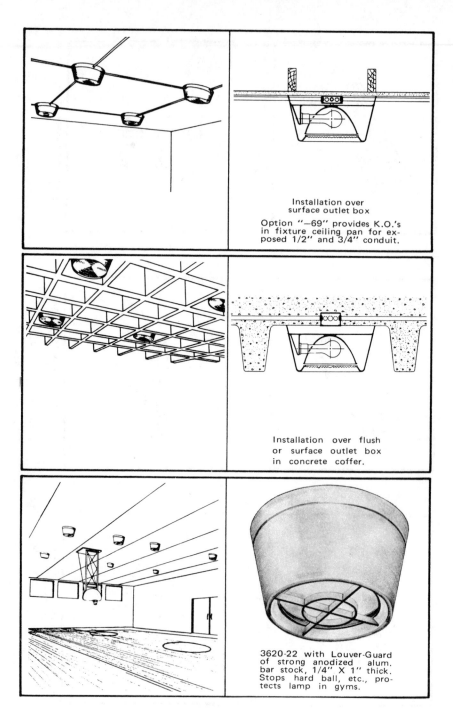

Installation over
surface outlet box

Option "—69" provides K.O.'s
in fixture ceiling pan for exposed 1/2" and 3/4" conduit.

Installation over flush
or surface outlet box
in concrete coffer.

3620-22 with Louver-Guard
of strong anodized alum.
bar stock, 1/4" X 1" thick.
Stops hard ball, etc., protects lamp in gyms.

Fig. 8–3.

TYPICAL INSTALLATION METHOD

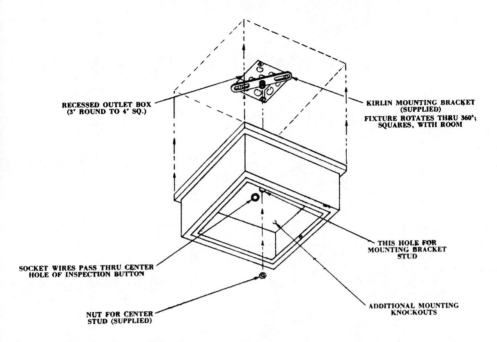

RECESSED OUTLET BOX
(3' ROUND TO 4' SQ.)

KIRLIN MOUNTING BRACKET
(SUPPLIED)
FIXTURE ROTATES THRU 360°;
SQUARES, WITH ROOM

THIS HOLE FOR
MOUNTING BRACKET
STUD

SOCKET WIRES PASS THRU CENTER
HOLE OF INSPECTION BUTTON

NUT FOR CENTER
STUD (SUPPLIED)

ADDITIONAL MOUNTING
KNOCKOUTS

TYPICAL TOP VIEW OF HOUSING

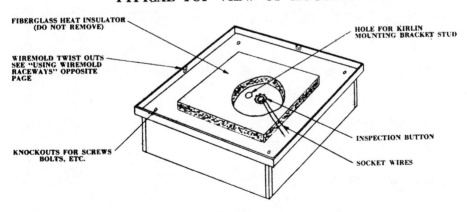

FIBERGLASS HEAT INSULATOR
(DO NOT REMOVE)

HOLE FOR KIRLIN
MOUNTING BRACKET STUD

WIREMOLD TWIST OUTS
SEE "USING WIREMOLD
RACEWAYS" OPPOSITE
PAGE

INSPECTION BUTTON

KNOCKOUTS FOR SCREWS
BOLTS, ETC.

SOCKET WIRES

Fig. 8–4.

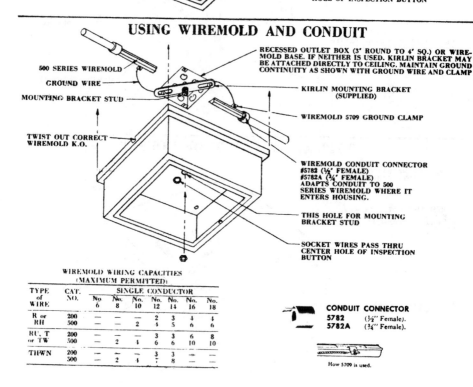

USING WIREMOLD RACEWAYS
(200 AND 500 SERIES)

NO-BOLT STUD

WIREMOLD BASE #5733, 5738, 5738A OR 5739 FOR USE WITH 500 SERIES. TO CONNECT 200 SERIES WIREMOLD TO A BASE USE 289A BASE AND A 289 REDUCING CONNECTOR

289A BASE

289

TWIST OUT CORRECT WIREMOLD K.O.

MAKE FIXTURE CONNECTION IN HOUSING

THIS HOLE FOR NO-BOLT STUD

SOCKET WIRES PASS THRU CENTER HOLE OF INSPECTION BUTTON

USING WIREMOLD AND CONDUIT

RECESSED OUTLET BOX (3″ ROUND TO 4″ SQ.) OR WIRE-MOLD BASE. IF NEITHER IS USED. KIRLIN BRACKET MAY BE ATTACHED DIRECTLY TO CEILING. MAINTAIN GROUND CONTINUITY AS SHOWN WITH GROUND WIRE AND CLAMP

500 SERIES WIREMOLD

GROUND WIRE

MOUNTING BRACKET STUD

KIRLIN MOUNTING BRACKET (SUPPLIED)

WIREMOLD 5709 GROUND CLAMP

TWIST OUT CORRECT WIREMOLD K.O.

WIREMOLD CONDUIT CONNECTOR #5782 (½″ FEMALE) #5782A (¾″ FEMALE) ADAPTS CONDUIT TO 500 SERIES WIREMOLD WHERE IT ENTERS HOUSING.

THIS HOLE FOR MOUNTING BRACKET STUD

SOCKET WIRES PASS THRU CENTER HOLE OF INSPECTION BUTTON

WIREMOLD WIRING CAPACITIES (MAXIMUM PERMITTED)

TYPE of WIRE	CAT. NO.	SINGLE CONDUCTOR						
		No. 6	No. 8	No. 10	No. 12	No. 14	No. 16	No. 18
R or RH	200	—	—	—	2	3	4	4
	500	—	—	2	4	5	6	6
RU, T or TW	200	—	—	—	3	3	6	8
	500	—	2	4	6	6	10	10
THWN	200	—	—	—	3	3	—	—
	500	—	2	4	7	8	—	—

CONDUIT CONNECTOR
5782   (½″ Female).
5782A (¾″ Female).

How 5709 is used.

Fig. 8–4. (cont'd)

NATL. ELEC. CODE REQUIREMENTS

REFER TO N.E.C. HAND BOOK FOR COMPLETE REQUIREMENTS

WIRING

410-65(A) Conductors having insulation suitable for the temperature encountered shall be used. *See table above or marking on housing.*
410-65(B) Fixtures having branch circuit terminal connections which operate at temperatures higher than 60°C. (140°F.) shall have circuit conductors as described in Sections 410-65 (B-1 and B-2).
410-65(B) (1) Branch Circuit Conductors having an insulation suitable for the temperature encountered may be run directly to the fixture.

or

410-65(B) (2) Tap Connection Conductors having an insulation suitable for the temperature encountered shall be run from the fixture terminal connection to an outlet box placed at least one foot from the fixture. Such a tap shall extend for at least 4 feet but not more than 6 feet and shall be in a suitable metal raceway.

CONNECTIONS, SPLICES AND TAPS

410-25(A) Fixtures shall be so installed that the connections between the fixture conductors and the circuit conductors may be inspected without requiring the disconnection of any part of the wiring, unless the fixture is connected by means of a plug and receptacle.

EQUIPMENT NEAR GROUNDED SURFACES

410-95(A) Ungrounded metal lighting fixtures, lamp holders and face plates shall not be installed in contact with conducting surfaces nor within 8 feet vertically or 5 feet horizontally of laundry tubs, bath tubs, shower baths, plumbing fixtures, steam pipes or other grounded metal work or grounded surfaces.

TRANSFORMER LOCATIONS

410-84(A) Transformers shall be accessible after installation.

AUXILIARY EQUIPMENT NOT INTEGRAL WITH FIXTURE

410-75(C) Ballasts approved for separate mounting and for direct connection to an approved wiring system need not be separately enclosed.

TEMPERATURE

410-63(A) Fixtures shall be so constructed or installed that adjacent combustible material will not be subjected to temperatures in excess of 90°C. (194°F.)

JUNCTION BOXES—THICKNESS OF METAL

370-20(B) For sheet steel boxes and fittings not over 100 cubic inches in size, the metal shall not be less than No. 14 USS Gauge (0.0747 in. in thickness).

Fig. 8–5.

REMODELING APPLICATIONS

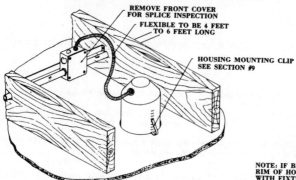

REMOVE FRONT COVER
FOR SPLICE INSPECTION

FLEXIBLE TO BE 4 FEET
TO 6 FEET LONG

HOUSING MOUNTING CLIP
SEE SECTION #9

NOTE

NOTE: IF BRASS TIARA AROUND
RIM OF HOUSING IS TO BE USED
WITH FIXTURES IT MUST BE
INSTALLED BEFORE HOUSING IS
INSERTED AND CONNECTIONS MADE

NOTE PRE-WIRED FIXTURES CAN BE INSERTED
FROM BELOW IF A HOLE SIZE OF 6¼ IS USED.
RIM OF HOUSING WILL COVER THE OPENING.

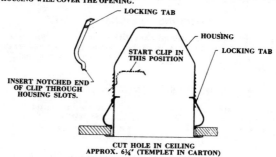

LOCKING TAB

HOUSING

START CLIP IN
THIS POSITION

LOCKING TAB

INSERT NOTCHED END
OF CLIP THROUGH
HOUSING SLOTS.

CUT HOLE IN CEILING
APPROX. 6¼″ (TEMPLET IN CARTON)

Fig. 8-5. (*cont'd*)

USE OF EYEBALL
#590, #591, #592

NOTE:
REMOVE SOCKET FROM REFLECTOR AND SNAP
IT ON THE EYEBALL IN THE POSITION SHOWN.
DISCARD THE REFLECTOR—DO NOT REINSTALL
IN THE HOUSING.

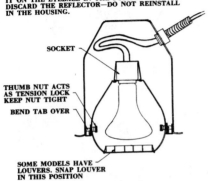

SOCKET

THUMB NUT ACTS
AS TENSION LOCK
KEEP NUT TIGHT

BEND TAB OVER

SOME MODELS HAVE
LOUVERS. SNAP LOUVER
IN THIS POSITION

MAXIMUM WATTAGE LAMP IS 110 WATT R-30

FOR EXTRA
VERTICAL ADJUSTMENT
WITH #400 MOUNTING FRAME

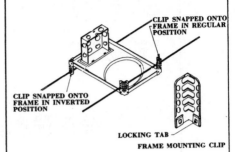

CLIP SNAPPED ONTO
FRAME IN REGULAR
POSITION

CLIP SNAPPED ONTO
FRAME IN INVERTED
POSITION

LOCKING TAB

FRAME MOUNTING CLIP

TO INSTALL DOMES
#416, #417

DOME CLIPS ARE PACKED
WITH THE DOME

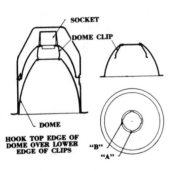

SOCKET

DOME CLIP

DOME

HOOK TOP EDGE OF
DOME OVER LOWER
EDGE OF CLIPS

"B"

"A"

TOP VIEW OF REFLECTOR

1. REMOVE SOCKET FROM NOTCHES "A"
2. INSERT DOME CLIPS IN NOTCHES "B"
3. REPLACE SOCKET WITH SOCKET
   CLIP IN NOTCHES "A"

TO INSTALL FRONT COVER

INSERT LOCATING TABS INTO
HOLES SHOWN. PRESS AT TOP
OF FRONT COVER AND LOCKING
TAB WILL ENGAGE BOX

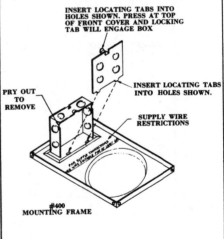

INSERT LOCATING TABS
INTO HOLES SHOWN.

PRY OUT
TO
REMOVE

SUPPLY WIRE
RESTRICTIONS

#400
MOUNTING FRAME

NOTE: DO NOT ATTEMPT TO
REMOVE BACK COVER

Fig. 8-5. (cont'd)

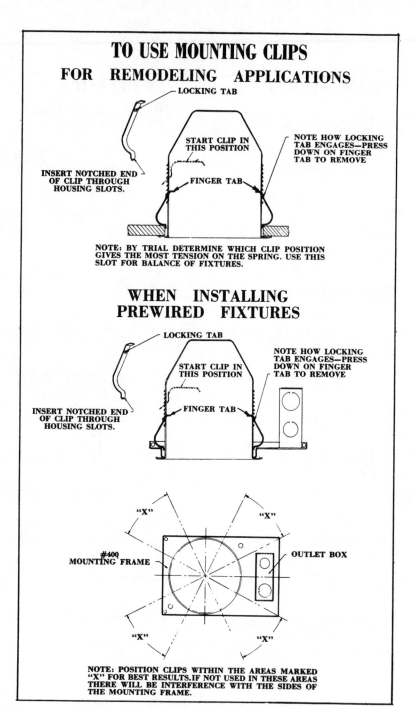

TO USE MOUNTING CLIPS
FOR REMODELING APPLICATIONS

LOCKING TAB

START CLIP IN THIS POSITION

NOTE HOW LOCKING TAB ENGAGES—PRESS DOWN ON FINGER TAB TO REMOVE

INSERT NOTCHED END OF CLIP THROUGH HOUSING SLOTS.

FINGER TAB

NOTE: BY TRIAL DETERMINE WHICH CLIP POSITION GIVES THE MOST TENSION ON THE SPRING. USE THIS SLOT FOR BALANCE OF FIXTURES.

WHEN INSTALLING PREWIRED FIXTURES

LOCKING TAB

START CLIP IN THIS POSITION

NOTE HOW LOCKING TAB ENGAGES—PRESS DOWN ON FINGER TAB TO REMOVE

INSERT NOTCHED END OF CLIP THROUGH HOUSING SLOTS.

FINGER TAB

"X"   "X"

#400 MOUNTING FRAME

OUTLET BOX

"X"   "X"

NOTE: POSITION CLIPS WITHIN THE AREAS MARKED "X" FOR BEST RESULTS. IF NOT USED IN THESE AREAS THERE WILL BE INTERFERENCE WITH THE SIDES OF THE MOUNTING FRAME.

Fig. 8-5. (cont'd)

TO INSTALL CONES
#410, #411, #413

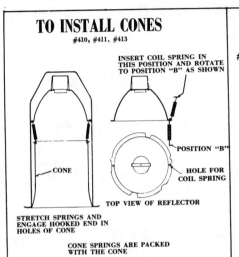

INSERT COIL SPRING IN
THIS POSITION AND ROTATE
TO POSITION "B" AS SHOWN

POSITION "B"

HOLE FOR
COIL SPRING

CONE

TOP VIEW OF REFLECTOR

STRETCH SPRINGS AND
ENGAGE HOOKED END IN
HOLES OF CONE

CONE SPRINGS ARE PACKED
WITH THE CONE

TO INSTALL GLOS, DOORS OR FLANGES
#402; #460 thru #488, #500 thru #522; #451, #452, #453

LOOP FOR DOOR
SPRING WIRE

SPRING WIRE—SQUEEZE
TO INSERT THROUGH
LOOP

TO INSTALL REFLECTORS

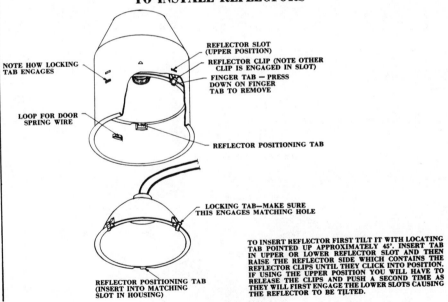

NOTE HOW LOCKING
TAB ENGAGES

REFLECTOR SLOT
(UPPER POSITION)

REFLECTOR CLIP (NOTE OTHER
CLIP IS ENGAGED IN SLOT)

FINGER TAB — PRESS
DOWN ON FINGER
TAB TO REMOVE

LOOP FOR DOOR
SPRING WIRE

REFLECTOR POSITIONING TAB

LOCKING TAB—MAKE SURE
THIS ENGAGES MATCHING HOLE

REFLECTOR POSITIONING TAB
(INSERT INTO MATCHING
SLOT IN HOUSING)

TO INSERT REFLECTOR FIRST TILT IT WITH LOCATING
TAB POINTED UP APPROXIMATELY 45°. INSERT TAB
IN UPPER OR LOWER REFLECTOR SLOT AND THEN
RAISE THE REFLECTOR SIDE WHICH CONTAINS THE
REFLECTOR CLIPS UNTIL THEY CLICK INTO POSITION.
IF USING THE UPPER POSITION YOU WILL HAVE TO
RELEASE THE CLIPS AND PUSH A SECOND TIME AS
THEY WILL FIRST ENGAGE THE LOWER SLOTS CAUSING
THE REFLECTOR TO BE TILTED.

Fig. 8-5. (*cont'd*)

KIRLIN DUAL PACK SYSTEM

ROUGH IN SECTION (HOUSING #700 THRU #795)

MAY BE PACKED AND PURCHASED TWO WAYS

PURCHASE MOUNTING FRAME #400 FIRST

PURCHASE UNWIRED HOUSING LATER

OR

PURCHASE PREWIRED HOUSING COMPLETE

FINISH SECTION (TRIMS #402 THRU #595)

SHOWN BELOW ARE BUT A FEW OF THE MANY FINISH SECTIONS THAT MAY BE PURCHASED AT A LATER DATE. ASSEMBLING THE FINISH SECTION TO THE ROUGH IN SECTION WILL RESULT IN A COMPLETE FIXTURE.

DOME   CONE   SLEEVE IN DOOR OR FLANGE   BOWL IN DOOR OR FLANGE   RECESSED FRESNEL IN DOOR OR FLANGE   GLO GLASS   EYEBALL IN DOOR OR FLANGE   GEM IN DOOR OR FLANGE

Fig. 8–5. (*cont'd*)

INVERTED TEE

(CONCEALED SYSTEM)

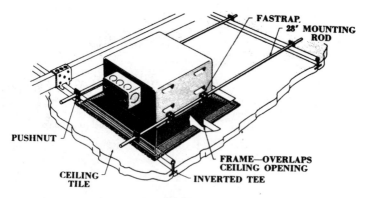

Fig. 8–6.

WET PLASTER

(PLASTER FRAMES MUST BE USED)

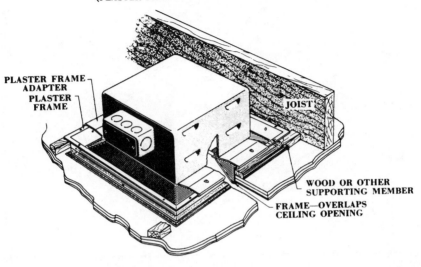

PLASTER FRAME
ADAPTER
PLASTER
FRAME

JOIST

WOOD OR OTHER
SUPPORTING MEMBER
FRAME—OVERLAPS
CEILING OPENING

"H" AND "T"

**(SHOWN WITH CEILING
RUNNERS ON 24" CENTERS)**

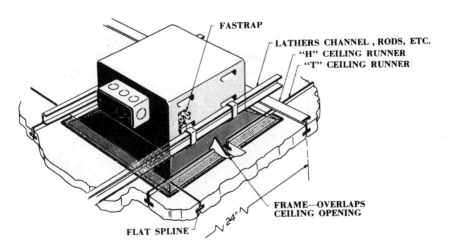

FASTRAP

LATHERS CHANNEL , RODS, ETC.
"H" CEILING RUNNER
"T" CEILING RUNNER

FLAT SPLINE

24"

FRAME—OVERLAPS
CEILING OPENING

Fig. 8–6. (*cont'd*)

SIMPLEX

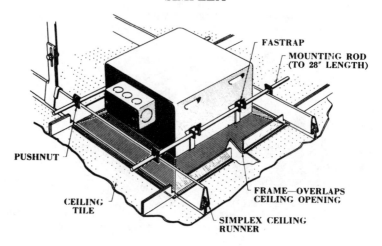

BURGESS MANNING

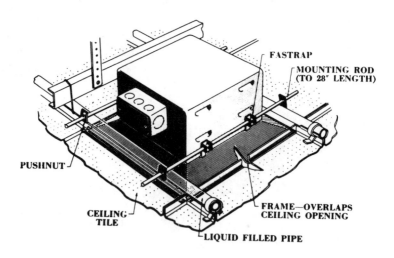

Fig. 8–6. (*cont'd*)

TEE BAR

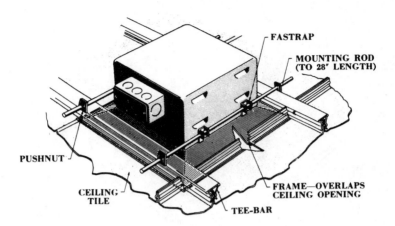

OTHER MOUNTING METHODS

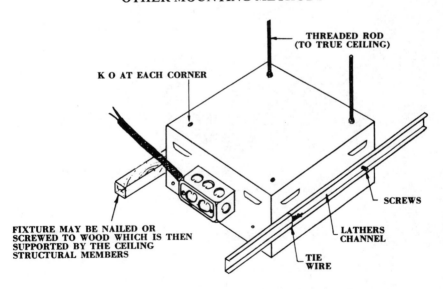

Fig. 8–6. (*cont'd*)

NAIL OR SCREW CHANNEL

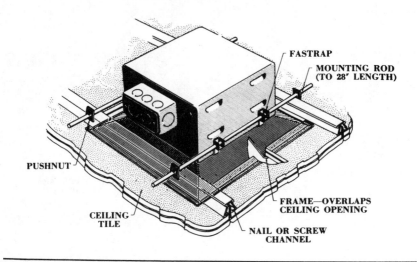

"Z" BAR

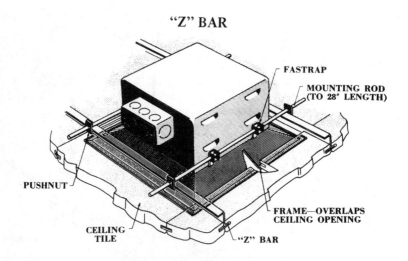

Fig. 8-6. (*cont'd*)

EXTRA WIRING CAPACITY

USING #111 ADAPTER

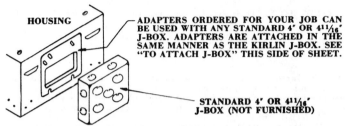

HOUSING

ADAPTERS ORDERED FOR YOUR JOB CAN BE USED WITH ANY STANDARD 4″ OR 4¹¹/₁₆″ J-BOX. ADAPTERS ARE ATTACHED IN THE SAME MANNER AS THE KIRLIN J-BOX. SEE "TO ATTACH J-BOX" THIS SIDE OF SHEET.

STANDARD 4″ OR 4¹¹/₁₆″ J-BOX (NOT FURNISHED)

USING EXTENSION RING

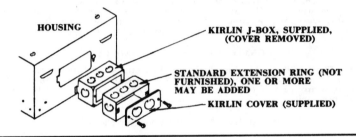

HOUSING

KIRLIN J-BOX, SUPPLIED, (COVER REMOVED)

STANDARD EXTENSION RING (NOT FURNISHED), ONE OR MORE MAY BE ADDED

KIRLIN COVER (SUPPLIED)

REMODELING

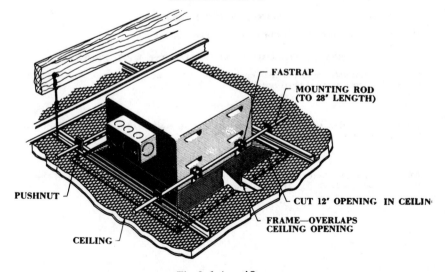

FASTRAP

MOUNTING ROD (TO 28″ LENGTH)

PUSHNUT

CUT 12″ OPENING IN CEILIN

FRAME—OVERLAPS CEILING OPENING

CEILING

Fig. 8-6. (*cont'd*)

NATL. ELEC. CODE REQUIREMENTS

REFER TO N.E.C. HAND BOOK FOR COMPLETE REQUIREMENTS

WIRING

410-65(A)   Conductors having insulation suitable for the temperature encountered shall be used. *See table above or marking on housing.*

410-65(B)   Fixtures having branch circuit terminal connections which operate at temperatures higher than 60°C. (140°F.) shall have circuit conductors as described in Sections 410-65 (B-1 and B-2).

410-65(B) (1)   Branch Circuit Conductors having an insulation suitable for the temperature encountered may be run directly to the fixture.

or

410-65(B) (2)   Tap Connection Conductors having an insulation suitable for the temperature encountered shall be run from the fixture terminal connection to an outlet box placed at least one foot from the fixture. Such a tap shall extend for at least 4 feet but not more than 6 feet and shall be in a suitable metal raceway.

CONNECTIONS, SPLICES AND TAPS

410-25(A)   Fixtures shall be so installed that the connections between the fixture conductors and the circuit conductors may be inspected without requiring the disconnection of any part of the wiring, unless the fixture is connected by means of a plug and receptacle.

EQUIPMENT NEAR GROUNDED SURFACES

410-95(A)   Ungrounded metal lighting fixtures, lamp holders and face plates shall not be installed in contact with conducting surfaces nor within 8 feet vertically or 5 feet horizontally of laundry tubs, bath tubs, shower baths, plumbing fixtures, steam pipes or other grounded metal work or grounded surfaces.

TRANSFORMER LOCATIONS

410-84(A)   Transformers shall be accessible after installation.

AUXILIARY EQUIPMENT NOT INTEGRAL WITH FIXTURE

410-75(C)   Ballasts approved for separate mounting and for direct connection to an approved wiring system need not be separately enclosed.

TEMPERATURE

410-63(A)   Fixtures shall be so constructed or installed that adjacent combustible material will not be subjected to temperatures in excess of 90°C. (194°F).

JUNCTION BOXES—THICKNESS OF METAL

370-20(B)   For sheet steel boxes and fittings not over 100 cubic inches in size, the metal shall not be less than No. 14 USS Gauge (0.0747 in. in thickness).

Fig. 8–7a.

WET PLASTER CEILINGS

WITHOUT PLASTER FRAMES

HOUSINGS WITH EARS OR K. O.'s
WITH MOUNTING RODS

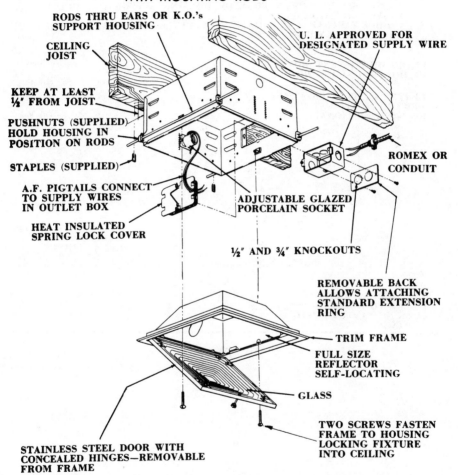

**RODS THRU EARS OR K.O.'s
SUPPORT HOUSING**

**CEILING
JOIST**

**U. L. APPROVED FOR
DESIGNATED SUPPLY WIRE**

**KEEP AT LEAST
½″ FROM JOIST**

**PUSHNUTS (SUPPLIED)
HOLD HOUSING IN
POSITION ON RODS**

STAPLES (SUPPLIED)

**ROMEX OR
CONDUIT**

**A.F. PIGTAILS CONNECT
TO SUPPLY WIRES
IN OUTLET BOX**

**ADJUSTABLE GLAZED
PORCELAIN SOCKET**

**HEAT INSULATED
SPRING LOCK COVER**

½″ AND ¾″ KNOCKOUTS

**REMOVABLE BACK
ALLOWS ATTACHING
STANDARD EXTENSION
RING**

TRIM FRAME

**FULL SIZE
REFLECTOR
SELF-LOCATING**

GLASS

**TWO SCREWS FASTEN
FRAME TO HOUSING
LOCKING FIXTURE
INTO CEILING**

**STAINLESS STEEL DOOR WITH
CONCEALED HINGES—REMOVABLE
FROM FRAME**

Fig. 8–7a. (cont'd)

WET PLASTER CEILINGS (cont'd)

USING FASTRAPS WITH MOUNTING RODS

TO INSTALL THE FIXTURE:
1. THREE FASTRAPS ARE POSITIONED ALONG EACH MOUNTING ROD.
2. THE TAIL OF FIRST AND THIRD FASTRAPS ARE BENT INWARD AND UP-WARD AROUND LOWER EDGE OF HOUSING SUPPORTING HOUSING ¼" ABOVE CEILING LINE.
3. MIDDLE FASTRAP (USE IS OPTIONAL) PREVENTS UPWARD MOVEMENT OF HOUSING WHEN USED AS SHOWN.

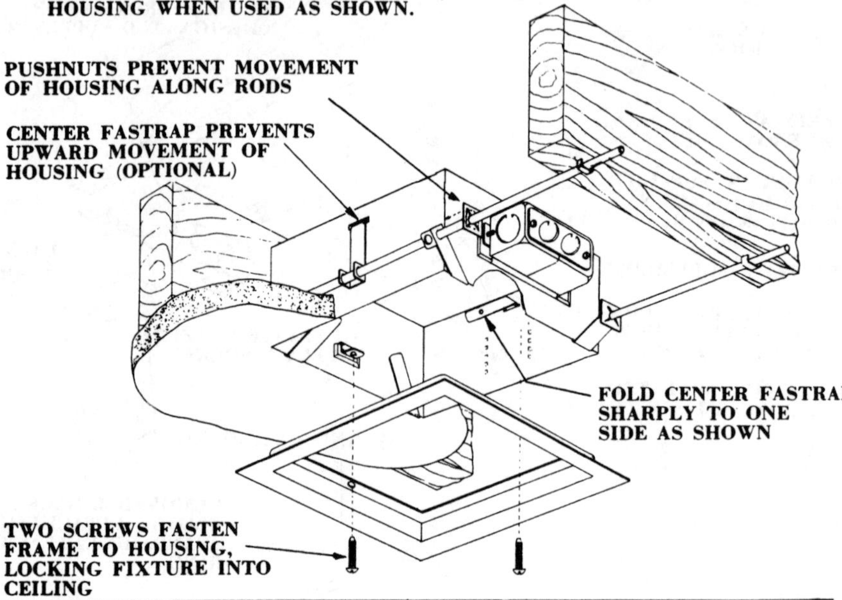

PUSHNUTS PREVENT MOVEMENT
OF HOUSING ALONG RODS

CENTER FASTRAP PREVENTS
UPWARD MOVEMENT OF
HOUSING (OPTIONAL)

FOLD CENTER FASTRAP
SHARPLY TO ONE
SIDE AS SHOWN

TWO SCREWS FASTEN
FRAME TO HOUSING,
LOCKING FIXTURE INTO
CEILING

Fig. 8–7a. (cont'd)

WITH PLASTER FRAMES

1. SNAP 4 SIDES TOGETHER (MOST MODELS—SEE SKETCH NO. 1).
2. LOCATE AND FASTEN FRAME IN CEILING. (ON 1511 AND 1508 MODELS ONE SIDE IS NOTCHED FOR J-BOX—POSITION NOTCH CORRECTLY).
3. BEND CLIPS DOWN, INSERT HOUSING, AND BEND CLIPS UP UNDER LOWER EDGE OF HOUSING. (SEE SKETCH NO. 2).
4. HOUSING IS LOCKED WHEN TRIM FRAME IS ASSEMBLED WITH SCREWS (SEE SKETCH NO. 3).

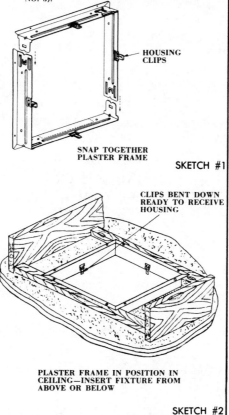

HOUSING CLIPS

SNAP TOGETHER PLASTER FRAME

SKETCH #1

CLIPS BENT DOWN READY TO RECEIVE HOUSING

PLASTER FRAME IN POSITION IN CEILING—INSERT FIXTURE FROM ABOVE OR BELOW

SKETCH #2

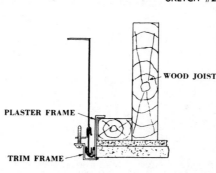

WOOD JOIST

PLASTER FRAME

TRIM FRAME

SKETCH #3

Fig. 8-7a. (*cont'd*)

KIRLIN DUAL PACKS

HOUSING PACK

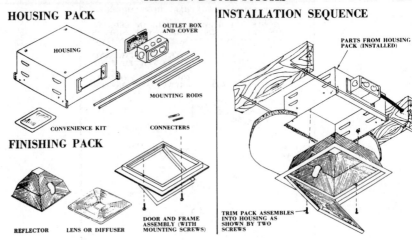

INSTALLATION SEQUENCE

OUTLET BOX AND COVER

HOUSING

MOUNTING RODS

CONVENIENCE KIT

CONNECTERS

PARTS FROM HOUSING PACK (INSTALLED)

FINISHING PACK

REFLECTOR   LENS OR DIFFUSER

DOOR AND FRAME ASSEMBLY (WITH MOUNTING SCREWS)

TRIM PACK ASSEMBLES INTO HOUSING AS SHOWN BY TWO SCREWS

REMODELING
USING FASTRAPS
WITHOUT USING MOUNTING EARS

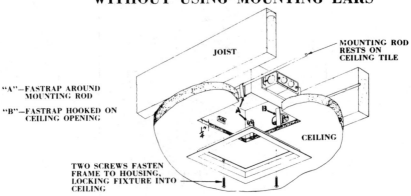

JOIST

MOUNTING ROD RESTS ON CEILING TILE

"A"—FASTRAP AROUND MOUNTING ROD

"B"—FASTRAP HOOKED ON CEILING OPENING

CEILING

TWO SCREWS FASTEN FRAME TO HOUSING, LOCKING FIXTURE INTO CEILING

USING MOUNTING EARS

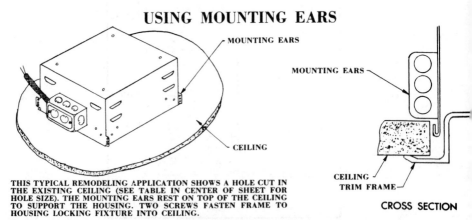

MOUNTING EARS

CEILING

MOUNTING EARS

CEILING
TRIM FRAME

CROSS SECTION

THIS TYPICAL REMODELING APPLICATION SHOWS A HOLE CUT IN THE EXISTING CEILING (SEE TABLE IN CENTER OF SHEET FOR HOLE SIZE). THE MOUNTING EARS REST ON TOP OF THE CEILING TO SUPPORT THE HOUSING. TWO SCREWS FASTEN FRAME TO HOUSING LOCKING FIXTURE INTO CEILING.

Fig. 8–7a. (cont'd)

CEILING OPENING SUPPLY WIRE LAMP SIZE

SQUARE RECESSED

Max. Rated Watts	Lamp	Cat. No.	Ceiling Opening	Depth	Supply Wire	Frame Dimen.
100	A-19	1207	7¾″ sq.	5⅛″	60°	8⅝″ sq.
150	A-21	1207Y*	7¾ sq.	5⅛	75°	8⅝ sq.
	A-21	1208	9⅜ sq.	5½	60°	10¼ sq.
	A-21	1508W	9⅜ sq.	3⅞	75°	10¼ sq.
200	A-23	1208Y*	9⅜ sq.	5½	75°	10¼ sq.
	PS-25	1211	11⅞ sq.	5⅝	60°	12⅞ sq.
	PS-25	1511	11⅞ sq.	4¼	60°	12⅞ sq.
	A-23	1611V	11⅞ sq.	9⅜	60°	12⅞ sq.
	A-23	1611VU	11⅞ sq.	9⅜	60°	12⅞ sq.
300	PS-25	1211Y*	11⅞ sq.	5⅝	75°	12⅞ sq.
	PS-30	1212	13¼ sq.	7⅝	60°	14⅛ sq.
	BT-28	1212 Hg.	13¼ sq.	7⅝	60°	14⅛ sq.
	PS-25	1611VY*	11⅞ sq.	9⅜	75°	12⅞ sq.
	PS-25	1611VYU*	11⅞ sq.	9⅜	60°	12⅞ sq.
	PS-35	1711V	11⅞ sq.	13¼	75°	12⅞ sq.
400 HG.		1218V Hg.	19⅜ sq.	15⅛	60°	20½ sq.
500	PS-35	1218V	19⅜ sq.	13⅛	60°	20½ sq.
750	PS-52	1218-750	19⅜ sq.	13⅛	90°	20½ sq.
1000	PS-52	1218-1000†	19⅜ sq.	13⅛	90°	20½ sq.

RECTANGULAR RECESSED

Max. Rated Watts	Lamp	Cat. No.	Ceiling Opening	Depth	Supply Wire	Frame Dimen.
50	A-19	508-NL	5⅝ x 8½	3	60°	6½ x 9⁷⁄₁₆
80-2/40	A-19	514	4½ x 14½	4¹⁄₁₆	75°	5¾ x 15¾
100	A-19	508	5⅝ x 8½	5⅞	60°	6½ x 9⁷⁄₁₆
150	PS-25	614	7⅝ x 13⅛	5¾	60°	8½ x 14⅛
200	PS-25	614-Y*	7⅝ x 13⅛	5¾	75°	8½ x 14⅛
300-2/150	PS-25	622	7¼ x 21¼	6⅝	75°	8¾ x 22⅝

*"Y" MODELS ARE IDENTICAL TO SAME FIXTURE WITH-OUT SUFFIX EXCEPT FOR U.L. MARKINGS.

†FOR FIRE RESISTANT CONSTRUCTION.

Fig. 8-7a. (*cont'd*)

FASTRAPS–SOLVE UNUSUAL PROBLEMS

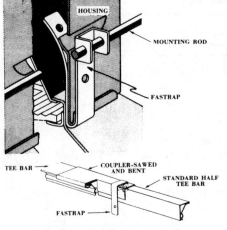

HOUSING

MOUNTING ROD

FASTRAP

IF YOUR CEILING CONDITIONS ARE NOT DETAILED ELSEWHERE ON THIS SHEET, THE FOLLOWING SUGGESTIONS MAY SOLVE YOUR PROBLEM. FASTRAPS ARE PROVIDED IN ADDITION TO STANDARD MOUNTING EARS, MOUNTING RODS, HOLES (FOR NAILS, SCREWS, AND TIE WIRES), AND KNOCKOUTS IN THE TOP OF HOUSING FOR RUNNING THREAD. TO USE FASTRAPS:

1. SECURE "TEE" END OF FASTRAP TO CEILING STRUCTURE (2 FASTRAPS ON EACH OF TWO OPPOSITE SIDES OF HOUSING).
2. LOCATE HOUSING ¼" TO ½" ABOVE FINISHED CEILING LINE AND BEND FASTRAPS AROUND LOWER EDGE OF HOUSING. SQUEEZE FASTRAPS TIGHTLY AGAINST SIDES OF HOUSING.
3. TWO ADDITIONAL FASTRAPS MAY BE INSERTED THRU HOLD DOWN SLOTS IN OPPOSITE SIDES OF HOUSING AND FOLDED OVER SHARPLY TO ONE SIDE LOCKING HOUSING DOWN.
4. TWO 10-24 SCREWS (UNDER GLASS CLIPS IN DOOR) DRAW FRAME UP INTO HOUSING. SNUGGLY AGAINST CEILING.

TEE BAR

COUPLER–SAWED AND BENT

STANDARD HALF TEE BAR

FASTRAP

THIS SHOWS A FASTRAP USED WITH A TEE BAR CEILING. IN THIS APPLICATION A HALF TEE BAR HAS BEEN USED TO PROVIDE A 12" CEILING OPENING.

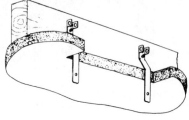

NAILED TO WOOD CEILING JOISTS

ATTACHED TO ENDS OF WIRES

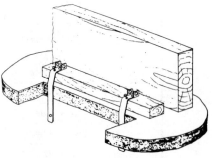

FASTRAPS NAILED TO A BLOCK OF WOOD

Fig. 8–7b. (*cont'd*)

MECHANICAL CEILINGS

RUNNERS NOT CUT

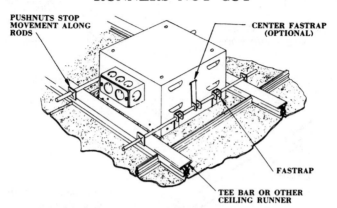

PUSHNUTS STOP
MOVEMENT ALONG
RODS

CENTER FASTRAP
(OPTIONAL)

FASTRAP

TEE BAR OR OTHER
CEILING RUNNER

RODS MAY BE CONNECTED TOGETHER TO FORM 28" MOUNTING RODS.
THESE ARE USED ON CEILINGS WHERE MAIN RUNNERS ARE ON 24" CENTERS.
SEE "MOUNTING RODS" THIS SIDE OF SHEET AND "FASTRAPS" ON
OPPOSITE SIDE. POSITION BOTTOM EDGE OF HOUSING ⅛" TO ¼" ABOVE
FINISHED CEILING LINE.

RUNNERS CUT—OPENING FRAMED

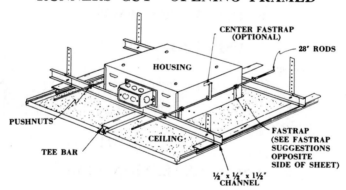

CENTER FASTRAP
(OPTIONAL)

28" RODS

HOUSING

PUSHNUTS

TEE BAR

CEILING

FASTRAP
(SEE FASTRAP
SUGGESTIONS
OPPOSITE
SIDE OF SHEET)

½" x ½" x 1½"
CHANNEL

IF REQUIRED, THE MOUNTING RODS MAY BE CONNECTED TOGETHER TO
FORM 28" RODS, SEE "MOUNTING RODS" THIS SIDE OF SHEET FOR IN-
STRUCTIONS. POSITION BOTTOM EDGE OF HOUSING ⅛" TO ¼" ABOVE
FINISHED CEILING LINE.

Fig. 8–7b. (cont'd)

MECHANICAL CEILINGS (*cont'd*)
INVERTED "TEE" OR GRID

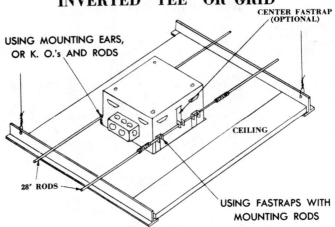

CENTER FASTRAP
(OPTIONAL)

USING MOUNTING EARS,
OR K. O.'s AND RODS

CEILING

28" RODS

USING FASTRAPS WITH
MOUNTING RODS

USE FASTRAPS AS SHOWN TO POSITION BOTTOM EDGE OF HOUSING ⅛"
TO ¼" ABOVE FINISHED CEILING LINE.

EXTRA WIRING CAPACITY

USING #4 ADAPTER

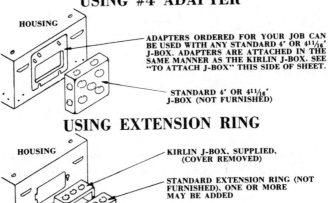

HOUSING

ADAPTERS ORDERED FOR YOUR JOB CAN
BE USED WITH ANY STANDARD 4" OR 4¹¹⁄₁₆"
J-BOX. ADAPTERS ARE ATTACHED IN THE
SAME MANNER AS THE KIRLIN J-BOX. SEE
"TO ATTACH J-BOX" THIS SIDE OF SHEET.

STANDARD 4" OR 4¹¹⁄₁₆"
J-BOX (NOT FURNISHED)

USING EXTENSION RING

HOUSING

KIRLIN J-BOX, SUPPLIED,
(COVER REMOVED)

STANDARD EXTENSION RING (NOT
FURNISHED), ONE OR MORE
MAY BE ADDED

KIRLIN COVER (SUPPLIED)

Fig. 8–7b. (*cont'd*)

FIXTURES IN PATTERNS

TYPICAL INSTALLATION
(4 GANG)

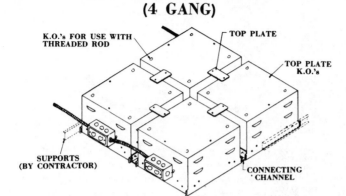

CONNECTING CHANNEL SET (FURNISHED)

ASSEMBLE AS SHOWN ABOVE AND BELOW WITH SCREWS PROVIDED. FIXTURES CONTAIN KNOCKOUTS FOR TOP PLATE SCREWS AND HOLES FOR CONNECTING CHANNEL SCREWS.

TYPICAL INSTALLATION
(2 GANG)

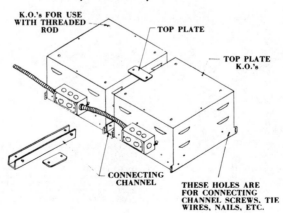

Fig. 8–7b. (*cont'd*)

FIXTURES IN CONCRETE TO INSTALL REFLECTORS

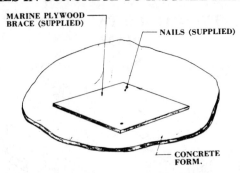

1. NAIL PLYWOOD BRACE TO CONCRETE FORM IN EXACT FIXTURE LOCATION.
2. DRIVE NAILS THROUGH MOUNTING EARS TO SECURE HOUSING TO FORM.
3. PLACE TAPE (PROVIDED) OVER CRACK BETWEEN J-BOX AND HOUSING.
4. POUR CONCRETE. CUT ENDS OF NAILS LEFT AFTER FORMS ARE STRIPPED.

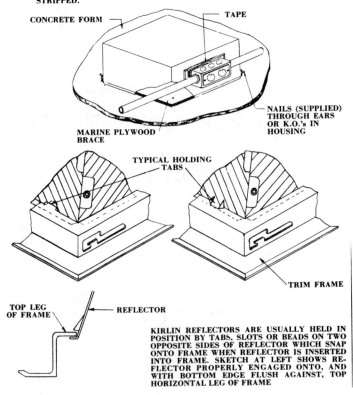

KIRLIN REFLECTORS ARE USUALLY HELD IN POSITION BY TABS, SLOTS OR BEADS ON TWO OPPOSITE SIDES OF REFLECTOR WHICH SNAP ONTO FRAME WHEN REFLECTOR IS INSERTED INTO FRAME. SKETCH AT LEFT SHOWS RE-FLECTOR PROPERLY ENGAGED ONTO, AND WITH BOTTOM EDGE FLUSH AGAINST, TOP HORIZONTAL LEG OF FRAME

Fig. 8–7b. (cont'd)

MOUNTING RODS

KIRLIN FIXTURES ARE PROVIDED WITH 4 MOUNTING RODS THAT
CAN BE CONNECTED TOGETHER TO PROVIDE TWO RODS 28″ LONG,
SPANNING CEILING RUNNERS ON 24″ CENTERS. ONE END OF A 10″
AND AN 18″ MOUNTING ROD ARE INSERTED INTO A TUBE CONNECTOR
WHICH LOCKS RODS TOGETHER.

10″ MOUNTING   HEAT TREATED   18″ MOUNTING
RODS   CONNECTORS   RODS

TO ADJUST SOCKETS

(WHEN SOCKET DOES NOT ALIGN WITH REFLECTOR HOLE)

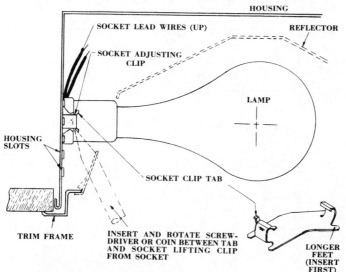

1. SNAP REFLECTOR FROM TRIM FRAME.
2. INSERT SCREWDRIVER OR COIN UNDER TABS OF SOCKET CLIP AND TWIST OUT.
3. REPOSITION CLIP BY INSERTING LONGER FEET FIRST INTO HOUSING SLOTS.
4. INSERT ONE SIDE OF SOCKET UNDER TAB END OF CLIP. SNAP SOCKET DOWN UNDER OPPOSITE END OF CLIP.

Fig. 8-7b. (cont'd)

OTHER MOUNTING METHODS

METHODS USED TO INSTALL KIRLIN FIXTURES ARE TOO NUMEROUS
TO DETAIL. A COMPOSITE OF COMMON METHODS IS SHOWN BELOW.

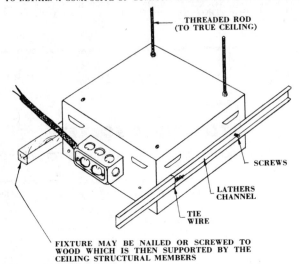

FIXTURE MAY BE NAILED OR SCREWED TO
WOOD WHICH IS THEN SUPPORTED BY THE
CEILING STRUCTURAL MEMBERS

TO INSTALL REMOVABLE DOORS

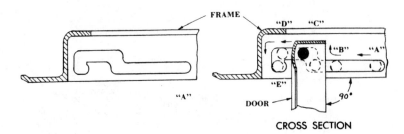

CROSS SECTION

1. WITH DOOR HELD PERPENDICULAR TO FRAME (AS SHOWN
   AT RIGHT) ENGAGE ONE DOOR HINGE PIN INTO SMALL
   OVAL HOLE IN SIDE WALL OF FRAME.

2. SLIP SECOND DOOR HINGE PIN HORIZONTALLY INTO "?"
   SLOT AT "A" IN OPPOSITE WALL OF FRAME MOVING DOOR
   THRU POSITIONS "B", "C", "D" TO "E" WHERE DOOR
   WILL CLOSE.

Fig. 8–7b. (cont'd)

TO INSTALL GLASS IN DOORS

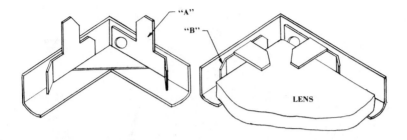

1. BEND TAB "A" ALLOWING LENS TO SLIP INTO DOOR
2. BEND TAB "A" DOWN SNUGGLY AGAINST LENS OR LOUVER
3. TWIST TAB "B" WITH THIN NOSE PLIERS CENTERING LENS IN DOOR

TO ATTACH J-BOX

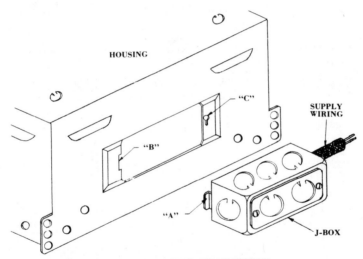

1. ENGAGE TAB "A" INTO NOTCH "B" OF HOUSING
2. POSITION SCREW OF OTHER TAB INTO KEYHOLE SLOT "C"
3. TIGHTEN SCREW TO SECURE BOX TO HOUSING

Fig. 8–7b. (*cont'd*)

UNWIRED FIXTURES

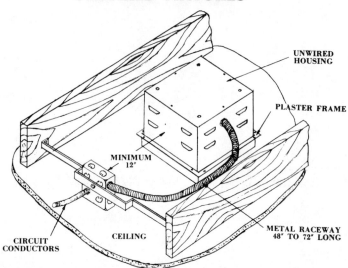

THE USE OF UNWIRED FIXTURES IS ADVANTAGEOUS IF THE EXACT LOCATION OF THE
FIXTURE HAS NOT BEEN DETERMINED IN ADVANCE. FIXTURES INSTALLED IN KIRLIN
PLASTER FRAMES OR BY USE OF FASTRAPS IN MECHANICAL CEILINGS MAY BE RE-
MOVED FROM THE CEILING, IF NECESSARY, FOR INSPECTION PURPOSES. REFER TO
THE NATIONAL ELECTRICAL CODE REQUIREMENTS SHOWN ON THE OTHER SIDE OF
THIS SHEET FOR WIRING REQUIREMENTS. UNWIRED FIXTURES VARY FROM WIRED
FIXTURES IN THAT THEY HAVE 54″ SOCKET LEADS AND NO ATTACHED J-BOX.

Fig. 8–7b. (*cont'd*)

Appendix I

Glossary

Illuminating engineering has emerged upon a new plateau with new horizons. Its integration into the environmental sciences has rapidly progressed among the related technologies. This integration and rapid advancement has made it necessary that those persons involved in the science of illumination revise and update their familiarity with terms that are now or will become common usage. With this purpose in mind, the following selection of engineering terminology is compiled. Some of the terms are new to all. Some have been redefined for clarity. Others are familiar terms to other sciences but are important for comprehension because of the integration of illumination with the structural and mechanical sciences. The list is by no means complete, nor could it remain complete for very long at the present rate of scientific growth. It is as authoritative and simple an explanation as can be formulated in a very complex and progressive technology.

Absolute Photometry: In photometric testing of luminaires, the procedure of calibrating the photometer head in terms of a working or primary standard of luminous intensity as opposed to relative photometry.

Absolute Zero: The temperature at which a system would undergo a reversible isothermal process without transfer of heat. The temperature at which an ideal gas would have zero volume. $-273.16°C$; $-459.69°F$; $0°K$.

Absorptance: The ratio of radiant flux absorbed by the body of a material to the radiant flux incident upon it. In photometric investigations the ratio would involve luminous flux.

Actinic Rays: Those wavelengths in the violet and ultraviolet region capable of effecting chemical changes, for example, fading of dyes and photography.

Acuity, Visual: The ability to distinguish fineness of detail. The test object used to evaluate this characteristic takes many shapes and forms. One of these is the Landolt ring. Another form has been used in the Blackwell investigations.

Ambient Noise Level: Stated in decibels, is the all-encompassing noise level associated with a given environment, being usually a composite of sounds from many sources and usually having no dominant frequency. In evaluating the noise level of a lighting system, it is that level of noise in a room when the lighting system is not in operation.

Ambient Temperature: The stable temperature of a surrounding medium such as of a lamp, luminaire, or a test mock-up. It is usually that point in distance from the test site at which there is no longer a temperature gradient.

Ampacity: A new term adopted by the National Electric Code specifying the capacity of an electrical conductor in amperes.

Angstrom: A unit of wavelength measurement; equals 10^{-8} centimeters. Visible light has a wavelength of 4000 to 7500 angstroms.

Anisotropic: Having different optical or other physical characteristics in different directions, e.g., wood will have different strengths with the grain as opposed to across the grain. Extruded plastics are usually stressed in the direction of the extrusion as opposed to cast sheet which is usually isotropic in character.

Annealing: The process of holding a solid material at elevated temperatures for a specified time to permit any metastable condition (strains, dislocations, vacancies) to be dispersed into thermodynamic equilibrium.

Anodizing: Any electrolytic or chemical process by which means a protective film is placed on a metal surface. A common process to both aluminum and magnesium.

Apostilb: Unit of luminance (brightness) equal to 1/1000 of a lambert.

Atmospheric Standard: Unit of pressure defined as the pressure exerted by a column of mercury 760 mm high having a density of 13.595 gm/cm^3 at sea level. Also referred to as *Absolute Pressure*.

Attenuation: In the most general sense, attenuation is reduction in concentration, density, or effectiveness. In acoustics, attenuation of sound is accomplished by absorption in many forms such as an increase in air humidity, properties of acoustical materials, and absorption by trees and bushes.

Average Luminance (average brightness): The luminance value of a luminaire (at a specified angle of view) expressed in candles per square inch or footlamberts. It is the average value of the luminous subtended area and is obtained by dividing the candlepower at the specified angle by the luminous subtended area of the luminaire. In the case of luminaires which depend upon secondary reflecting, surfaces may be taken into account under controlled conditions in the calculations. Average luminance values are calculated from related data as opposed to maximum luminance values which are measured.

Baffle: In luminaire design, a blade of opaque or semi-opaque material used primarily to control the light distribution or shield the lamp.

Ballast: Essentially an electromagnetic device used with electrical discharge lamps to control operating and starting conditions for optimum lamp performance.

Black Body: Theoretically a full radiator, one which absorbs all incident radiation, reflecting none. Such a body will emit radiation in which the energy contained in any frequency range is related with that frequency and with that temperature of the radiator, according to Planck's equation for black body radiation.

Black Light: A term used for ultraviolet radiation near the visible spectrum. A fluorescent lamp without its normal phosphor coatings is an efficient generator of black light or ultraviolet energy.

Brewester Angle: Polarizing angle of material is that angle of incidence for which a wave polarized parallel to the plane of incidence is wholly transmitted with no reflections. The relationship is that the tangent of the polarizing angle is equal to the refractive index of the material as stated in Brewester's Law.

Brightness: See Subjective Brightness and Luminance.

Brightness Coefficients: See Luminance Coefficients.

Brightness Ratios: See Luminance Ratios.

British Thermal Unit: Unit of energy abbreviated Btu; the energy required to raise the temperature of one pound of water $1°F$ with no vaporization. In air-conditioning design data it is utilized as btu per hour. Electrical equivalent =.293 watts.

Calorimeter: A device for measuring the change of heat content of a system.

Candela: Unit of luminous intensity, one candela is equal to 1/60 of one square centimeter of projected area of a black body radiator operating at the freezing point of platinum.

Candle: Same as Candela.

Candlepower: Luminous intensity expressed in candelas. In the early days of photometry, luminous intensity was measured by rating sources in terms of ordinary candles. With the advent of more precise standards of luminous intensity, more precise measurements are possible through the use of the standard candle in terms of the luminous intensity of a black body radiator at the temperature of freezing platinum.

Cathode: An electrode where positive current leaves a device which employs electrical conduction other than through solids, such as electrical discharge lamps. A fluorescent lamp has an electrode at each end that serves as a cathode or anode, depending upon the alternations in the current.

Cavity Ratios: A number indicating cavity proportions calculated from length, width and height.

C.B.M.: Certified Ballast Manufacturer.

Ceiling Cavity: The cavity formed by the ceiling, the plane of the luminaires, and the wall surfaces between that plane and the ceiling.

Chromaticity of a Color: The dominant or complementary wavelength and purity aspects of a color taken together, or the aspects specified by chromaticity coordinates of the color taken together.

Chromaticity Coordinates: of a light—x, y, z: The ratios of each of the tristimulus values.

C.I.E. (Commission Internationale de l'Eclairage): The International Commission on Illumination.

Coefficients of Utilization: Ratio of luminous flux (lumens) received on the work plane to the rated lumens of the lamp or lamps.

Cold Cathode Lamp: An electrical discharge lamp designed to start without the need to preheat electrodes, e.g., "Slimline" and "Instant Start" lamps.

Color Temperature: The temperature at which the light from a black body radiator matches, in chromaticity, the light from the given source.

Contrast: Also Luminance Contrast. The difference in luminance between the background and the object, divided by the background luminance, where the background area is larger than the object.

Cosine Law; A distribution of flux such that the flux per unit solid angle in any direction from a plane surface varies as the cosine of the angle between that direction and the perpendicular to that surface.

CU: Coefficient of Utilization, sometimes written KU.

Decibel: A unit of sound level expressing the ratio of two amounts of power. The number of decibels denoting such a ratio is 10 times the logarithm to the base ten of the ratio

$$DB = 10 \log_{10} \frac{P1}{P2}$$

Diffuser: A device to redirect or scatter the light from a source. It may do so by diffuse reflection or diffuse transmission. In luminaire design, the device is primarily utilized for diffuse transmission.

Direct Glare: Glare resulting from high brightness in the field of view from luminaires or from reflecting surfaces acting as secondary light sources.

Disability Glare: Glare that reduces visual performance and visibility and is often accompanied by discomfort.

Discomfort Glare: Glare that produces discomfort; it does not necessarily interfere with visual performance or visibility.

Effective Ceiling Cavity Reflectance: See Chapter 6 on Illuminating Calculations.

Effective Floor Cavity Reflectance: See Chapter 6 on Illuminating Calculations.

Efficacy, Luminous: Related to light sources as the ratio of total lumens to the total power input, usually in watts.

Electric Discharge Lamps: Any lamp in which radiant energy in or near the visible spectrum is produced by the passage of arc current through a vapor or gas, e.g., fluorescent, neon, and mercury vapor lamps.

Fire Rating: A term used in the investigation of structures and assemblies regarding their fire resistance. Structures and assemblies are classified on a time basis as an indication of their ability to resist the passage or propagation of flames from one area to another or to material of lesser resistance to fire. In this aspect, assemblies refer to those assembled on the construction site employing techniques normally associated with the building industry and utilizing recognized or approved materials and components.

Flame Spread Rating: A term used in the investigation of materials in regards to fire hazard. Underwriter's Laboratories, Inc. (U.L.), classify such materials in comparison to asbestos cement boards as 0 and red oak lumber as 100 when exposed to fire under similar conditions.

Floor Cavity: The cavity formed by the floor, the work plane (usually 30 inches above the floor), and the wall surfaces between work plane and floor.

Fluorescence: The process of emission of electromagnetic radiation by a substance as the result of absorption of energy from some other electromagnetic or particulate radiation, provided that the emission continues only as long as the stimulus that produces the emission is maintained.

Flux, Luminous: The time rate of flow of luminous radiation.

Flux Density: Luminous flux per unit area of the surface.

Flux Transfer Theory: An analytical method of determining the flux distribution within an enclosure. The basic theory of application is derived from earlier established data utilized in thermodynamic studies of the distribution of radiant energy at other wavelengths.

Footcandle: The unit of illumination on a surface when the foot is the unit of length. It equals one lumen per square foot, provided that the luminous flux is distributed uniformly over that area.

Footlambert: A unit of luminance equal to one candle per square foot or to the uniform luminance of a perfectly diffusing surface emitting or reflecting light at the rate of one lumen per square foot. Since all surfaces absorb some portion of the light incident on them, the footcandles on a uniformly diffuse reflecting surface multiplied by its reflection factor is the luminance of that surface in footlamberts.

Footpound: A unit of work or energy; the work done when an average force of one pound produces a displacement of one foot in the direction of the force.

Form Factor: A number; a percentage of the total luminous flux from a surface A that falls on another surface B. The form factor is an essential element in the theory of flux transfer within enclosures such as rooms.

Fovea: A depressed area in the retina located in the direct line of sight through the lens system of the eye.

Freezing Point: The temperature at which the liquid state of a material becomes a solid. This is not always the same as the melting point of the solid. Since the freezing point varies with pressure, the pressure should be stated in recording data. Atmospheric pressure is commonly understood unless specified otherwise.

Fresnel Lens: A design method of simple lenses whereby the weight, size, and cost of a lens may be reduced but retains the optical action.

General Diffuse: C.I.E. distribution classification for luminaires having flux distribution of 40-60% above and 40-60% below the horizontal with considerable distribution horizontally as opposed to the direct/indirect distribution classification with little or no horizontal distribution.

Glare: A general term used to describe the sensation produced by luminances within the visual field that are sufficiently greater than the luminance to which the eyes are adapted; to cause annoyance, discomfort, or loss in visual performance or visibility.

Glare Factor: An index of glare sensation, or a glare rating for lighting systems. Such a method of predicting discomfort glare depends upon the type and number of luminaires used, their placement, the room size, and the reflectances of ceilings, walls, and floors.

Gloss: The characteristic produced by the high specular reflectivity in proportion to the diffuse reflectivity of surfaces.

Halogen: One of a family of elements such as iodine, bromine, fluorine, and chlorine, which combine directly with metals to produce halides. The use of iodine in incandescent lamps to improve life characteristics has identified such lamps as halogen lamps.

Hazardous Locations: As defined by the National Electric Code is an area involving an atmosphere containing inflammable dusts, vapors, or gases in explosive concentrations, which may be hazardous to public life and property. Equipment including luminaires for use in such areas is designed to meet the requirements for such applications, depending upon the classification of such a hazardous area. These classifications are covered in the NEC.

Heat: A form of Kinetic Energy, associated with the random agitation of molecules within a substance or material. It is customary to express heat quantitatively by means of British thermal units or calories. In thermodynamic calculations it is necessary to use the mechanical equivalent of heat as a conversion factor between these and ordinary dynamic units, e.g., footpounds.

Heat, Mechanical Equivalent of: A conversion factor between a unit of electrical energy and a unit of thermal energy.
1 watt = 3.414 Btu per hour
1 watt = .2389 g–cal. per second

Heat, Sensible: In air conditioning design, in determining the total heat load in an environmental space, one of the factors is that portion of heat gain from equipment. Any source of energy which changes the temperature is termed Sensible Heat.

Heat Transfer: Heat can be transferred by three methods: conduction, radiation and convection. The last method is sometimes referred to as Dynamic Conduction.

Heat Transfer Coefficient: Rate of heat flow through a medium, or a system expressed as the amount of heat through unit area, per unit time and per degree temperature difference. Commonly expressed in Btu square feet per hour per $^\circ$F.

Horsepower: Rate of performing work. 1 H.P. = 550 footpounds per second or 746 watts.

Hue: The attribute of color perception that determines whether it is red, yellow, green, and so forth. A subjective term corresponding to the psychophysical term Dominant Wavelength.

Hygrometer: An instrument used to determine the absolute or relative water content of air. A common type is the psychrometer.

Illumination: The luminous flux received by a surface per unit area of that surface. The unit of illumination is the footcandle or lumens per square foot.

Incandescence: The emission of visible radiant energy by a heated body which may be a solid, liquid, or gas. The temperature of a body required to produce incandescence will vary depending upon the material. Excitation to produce incandescence can be achieved by several means. In lighting, the effect is produced by the passage of an electrical current as in an incandescent lamp.

Incidence, Angle of: The angle at which radiation strikes a surface, measured from a line perpendicular to the surface to the line of direction of the radiation.

Index, Color Rendering (C.R.I.): A method of measuring and specifying the color-rendering properties of light sources as proposed by the C.I.E. These ratings are in terms of a single index—R. A lamp with C.R.I. of 100 would have color-rendering properties identical to those of a standard reference lamp. A lamp with a C.R.I. of 60, for example, would have color-rendering properties that shift the colors of illuminated objects about equal to that of a standard white flourescent lamp at 3000°K in comparison to the color of illuminated objects under an incandescent lamp at 3000°K.

Infrared Radiation: Radiant energy lying in the spectrum band between .75 microns and 10000 microns. Sometimes subdivided into Near infrared (.75 to 3 microns), Middle infrared (3 to 30 microns), and Far infrared (30 to 1000 microns).

Index of Refraction: The velocity of light in a vacuum divided by the velocity of the same light in a specific medium. In optics this ratio is usually defined as velocity in air to the velocity through the medium.

Intensity, Luminous: Same as Candlepower.

Inter-Reflectance: Also Interflectance. The portion of the lumens reaching the work plane that has been reflected one or more times from the room surfaces as determined by the Flux Transfer Theory.

Inverse Square Law: As applied to illumination, states that the illumination at a point on a surface varies directly with the candlepower and inversely as the square of the distance between the source and the point. This law holds true where the distance between source and point is at least five times maximum dimension of the source.

Iso Footcandle Diagram: Also Isolux Diagram. A series of lines, each of equal footcandle values. For a complete exploration, each line is a closed curve.

Isotherm Diagram: A series of lines each of equal temperature values. For complete exploration, each line is a closed curve.

Isotropic: A characteristic of a material whose properties are the same in whatever direction they are measured, as contrasted to anisotropic.

Joule: A unit of energy or work in the MKS system of units.
$$1 \text{ joule} = 10^{-7} \text{ ergs} = .2390 \text{ calories}$$

Lambert: A unit of luminance $= 1/\text{candle per cm}^2$ and therefore equal to the luminance of a perfectly diffusing surface emitting or reflecting light at the rate of one lumen per square centimeter.

Lambert Cosine Law: The intensity from a source of perfectly diffusing distribution is proportional to the cosine of the angle between the direction of emission and the normal to that surface. A source that obeys this law will appear equally bright from any direction.

Lambert Emitter: A source having the same luminance or brightness from any angle of view and therefore obeying the Lambert Cosine Law.

LDD (Luminaire Dirt Depreciation): A factor utilized in illumination computations to predict the reduction in initial illumination based upon the type of lamp and the relamping program to be used.

Lumen: The unit of luminous flux. It is equal to the flux through a unit solid angle (steradian) from a uniform point source of one candela (candle).

Lumen Maintenance: A term applied to data usually presented in graph form illustrating a lamp's ability to produce rated lumens throughout its rated life.

Lumen Method: A method of calculation to predict the average illumination on a work plane in a room. The maximum and minimum values of illumination will depend upon type of luminaire selected and their placement within a room. All calculations assume that the principles of good lighting layout are applied and that the conditions such as voltage, temperature, etc., will permit luminaires to provide their rated output.

Luminaire Classification: Luminaires are classified for general lighting by the C.I.E. in accordance with the percentage of total luminaire output emitted above and below horizontals.

Luminance: The current accepted term for brightness. The quantitative attribute of light that correlates with the sensation of brightness; it is the evaluation of radiance by means of the standard luminosity function. In photometric practice, it is the luminous flux per unit of projected area and unit solid angle, either leaving a surface at a given point in a given direction or arriving at a surface at a given point from a given direction; the luminous intensity of a surface in a given direction per unit of projected area of the surface as viewed from that direction. The units of luminance commonly utilized are candelas (candles) per square inch and footlamberts.

Luminance Coefficients: A coefficient, similar to the Coefficient of Utilization, used to predict the average luminance of room surfaces.

Luminance Contrast: See Contrast.

Luminance Factor: The ratio of the luminance of a surface or medium under specified conditions of incidence, observation, and light source to the luminance of a Lambert Emitter under the same conditions. Reflectance or transmittance cannot exceed unity, but the Luminance Factor can have any value between zero to values approaching infinity.

Luminance Ratios: The ratio between any two areas in the visual field.

Luminous Efficacy: See Mechanical Equivalent of Light.

Lux: The unit of illumination when the meter is the unit of length; equal to one lumen per square meter. The phot is the unit of illumination per square centimeter.

Maintenance Factor: The product of the Lamp Lumen Depreciation Factor (LLD) and the Luminance Dirt Depreciation Factor (LDD).

$$LLD \times LDD = MF$$

Magnalium: An alloy of magnesium and aluminum which has high reflectivity in the visible and ultraviolet regions.

Manometer: An instrument for measuring pressure. Usually, some form of liquid manometer using the pressure produced by a liquid column to balance the pressure to be measured. Some common types are: U-tube, inclined, well-type, and McLeod gauge.

Matte Surface: A surface from which the reflection is predominantly diffuse with or without a negligible specular component.

Mechanical Equivalent of Light: The maximum luminous efficacy of radiation is 682 lumens per watt. A theoretical value derived from the spectral distribution of a full radiator at the temperature of freezing platinum. The maximum value is calculated for green light of 555 nanometers in wavelength and to which wavelength the eye is most sensitive. The maximum possible efficacy of an ideal white light is roughly 200 lumens per watt and represents the practical limit in lamp efficacy that can be reached.

Millimicron: A unit of wavelength equal to one-billionth of a meter, superseded by the nanometer to which it is equal.

Mounting Height: (a) The distance from the work plane to the light center of the luminaire or to the plane of the ceiling in recessed application. The work plane is denoted as a horizontal plane 30 inches above the room floor. This dimension is also the height of the Room Cavity. (b) The distance from the floor to the light center of the luminaire or to the plane of the ceiling in recessed application.

Mounting Method: Conventional interpretation for types of luminaire mounting are not in agreement with those defined by various codes. Generally speaking, regardless of the type of ceiling, a luminaire mounted into a ceiling or wall cavity is said to be a recessed fixture. A surface-mounted luminaire would be mounted directly to such a ceiling or wall. A suspended luminaire would be hung to the ceiling by supports or stems. For purposes of illumination design, these interpretations are adequate.

According to the NEC and the U.L.'s requirements for Lighting Fixtures, the generalized description as stated is not adequate and does not meet with the intent of electrical codes. The ceiling, as it is known in the building trades, is of two basic types: (a) a *structural* ceiling and (b) a *suspended* ceiling. A suspended ceiling may be luminous or non-luminous. The space between a structural ceiling and a suspended ceiling is termed the *ceiling plenum*. According to the generalized interpretation, all fixtures within the ceiling cavity could be termed recessed or flush mounted, which is not true. Due to the complexity of luminaire classification to meet the requirements of safety to public life and property, the reader is referred to the NEC and U.L.'s Standards for Electric Lighting Fixtures for essential information about mounting classification.

Nanometer: A unit of wavelength equal to one-billionth of a meter, replaces millimicron to which it is equal.

National Electric Code (NEC): One of ten volumes of the National Fire Codes. A compilation of the codes, standards, recommended practices, and manuals devoted to the reduction of loss of life and property due to fire. They are purely advisory in nature, but are adopted widely by authorities having jurisdiction in enforcing regulations governing the proper use of electrical equipment and material.

Nema: National Electric Manufacturers Association.

Nephelometer: An instrument used in photometry for determining the amount of light transmitted or scattered by a suspension of particles.

Neutral Density Filter: A light filter which reduces the intensity of the light without changing the relative spectral distribution.

Nichol Prism: A device used to produce plane-polarized light constructed of two pieces of Iceland spar, cut in a precise manner and cemented together with Canada balsam causing double refraction to unpolarized light. This produces an ordinary and extraordinary ray, the latter being plane polarized upon exit from the prism.

Night Blindness: If the fovea of the eye has no rods, that part of the retina suffers from night blindness, a term describing various degrees of inability to see with low illumination.

Noise: Any undesired sound. By extension, noise is any unwanted disturbance within a useful frequency band such as undesired electrical waves in any transmission channel or device. Such disturbances when produced by other services are called *interference*. For example, the noise produced by a ballast as compared to the interference produced by the fluorescent lamp.

Noise Level: The value of noise integrated over a specified frequency range with a specified frequency weighting and integration time. It is expressed in decibels relative to a specified reference.

Normal: Perpendicular to a line. In illumination of a light, ray is normal to a surface when its direction of propagation is perpendicular to the plane of the surface at the point of incidence.

NRC (Noise Reduction Coefficient): NRC of a material is the average to the nearest multiple of .05 of the absorption coefficients, at 250, 500, 1000, and 2000 cycles.

Null: Zero, or without action or in the case of an instrument, without giving a reading.

Octave: The interval between two sounds having a basic frequency ratio of two.

Ocular: A lens through which anything is viewed. Commonly the lens in an optical instrument in the end through which the image is viewed by the eye.

Opacity: Imperviousness to radiation, especially to light. The reciprocal of the transmittance. Density is the logarithm of opacity to the base 10.

Opal Glass: A white diffusing glass material.

Optometry: A branch of optics dealing with the optical performance of the eye and with measurements upon it.

Orifice: An opening through which a fluid or gas may be discharged.

Orifice Plate: A diaphragm inserted in a pipe along which a fluid or a gas is flowing. If the orifice plate is sharp-edged, the pressure drop across it is proportional to the square of the flow through the pipe.

Ozone-Producing Lamps: Lamps producing ultraviolet energy shorter than about 220 nanometers which decompose oxygen and produce ozone.

Parabolic Reflector: A reflector for controlling light rays employing the property of the parabola to redirect a light ray originated at the focal point in a direction parallel to the axis.

Pencil (of Light): A homocentric bundle or rays corresponding to a train of concentric waves.

Pendant Mounting: In application, a luminaire suspended below a ceiling by means of stems, rods, or other suspension devices. According to UL requirements, the length of suspension must be at least 6 inches from the ceiling to classify as a pendant or suspended luminaire.

Phon: Unit of the loudness level of sound defined as numerically equal to the sound pressure level in decibels relative to .0002 microbar of a simple tone of frequency 2000 cycles per second which is judged by the listeners to be equivalent in loudness.

Phonetics: The science of speech.

Phosphor: Any substance which exhibits luminescence.

Phosphorescence: Luminescence which is delayed by more than 10^{-8} seconds after excitation. It may be associated with transitions from a higher excited state to a lower one.

Phosphotizing: In paint finishing of steel, the process of applying a phosphate coating by chemical means to prevent or delay the oxidation or rusting of steel.

Phot: A unit of luminance equal to one lumen per square centimeter.

Photochemical Effect: A chemical process initiated by radiant energy. The radiation may be in any portion of the spectrum, depending upon the type of chemical process involved. Examples of the photochemical processes are: blueprint machines, photography, photocopying and the visual response generated in the eye by the photochemical process in the rods and coes.

Photoconductive Effect: The increase in conductivity in many materials, particularly crystals under the action of light.

Photoelectric Effect: In its earlier use, this term covers broadly all changes in electrical characteristics of substances due to radiation, generally in the form of light. Currently, the photoconductive and photovoltaic effects in their narrower meaning are not included and are defined separately. The term *photoelectric effect* is restricted to the photoemissive effect.

Photopic Vision: In the eye, when only the cones in the fovea are involved, such as at the high illumination levels.

Photosynthesis: The process in plants of the manufacture of carbohydrates from carbon dioxide and water in the presence of light, through the mechanism of chlorophyll.

Photovoltaic Effect: The production of an electromotive force by the action of radiant energy commonly light upon the function of two dissimilar materials. A photovoltaic cell of the barrier layer type of certain metal semiconductors are common examples of this action.

Pitot Tube: An open-ended tube, pointing directly into the flow of a fluid or gas and connected to a manometer. The Pitot tube is often combined with a static pressure tube and connected to a differential manometer. The pressure difference measured is the dynamic pressure, and from this the flow velocity may be computed.

Planck Law of Distribution: The fundamental law of the quantum theory expressing the essential concept that energy transfers associated with radiation such as light are made up of definite quanta or increments of energy proportional to the frequency of the corresponding radiation. The constant of proportionality is known as *Planck's Constant*.

Planckian Radiator: A complete radiator, a black body radiator, basically a radiator having a spectral distribution of energy according to Planck's Law of Distribution.

Plastics: A general term relating to synthetic organic materials of high molecular weight. Plastics are broadly classified as thermosetting or thermoplastic types, and are available in clear, translucent, or opaque transmissions and by the addition of color pigments or dyes, produced in a variety of colors. Their use in luminaire and lighting design is steadily increasing and in many cases of vital importance.

Point by Point Calculations: In predicting illumination at a point, methods for average calculations cannot be used, and point by point procedures must be substituted. Since such methods do not account for interreflections within enclosures, the results are usually lower than those actually produced.

Polar Coordinates: A system of coordinates in which one ordinate is the distance from a center and the other ordinate is the amount of angular displacement around that center from some radial line as the reference. In photometric distribution presentation the line of reference at $0°$ is usually placed in the direction of Nadir, being in a direction directly below the center of a circle as opposed to Zenith as directly above and opposite in direction. The horizontal plane would then be a line at the $90°$ and $270°$ points through the center of such a circle.

Polarization: The process by which the transverse vibrations of light waves are oriented in a specific plane or the process of confining the magnetic or electric field vector of light or other radiation to one dominant plane. Light consists of electromagnetic waves with their electric and magnetic vectors constantly normal to the direction of propagation of the light beam. If the electric vectors of all components of a light beam lie in the same fixed plane, the light is said to be *plane polarized.* For purposes of orientation identification, the direction of the vectors are related so that the two orthogonal planes are either horizontal or vertical—although in unpolarized light there will be components between these dominant planes of vibrations. Multilayer polarizers by arrangement of their flakes or crystals can eliminate or retard the horizontal plane of vibrations and individually produce a cone of light rays with a dominant, vertically polarized component which is greatest at Brewster's angle and zero at normal incidence. The multilayer polarizer is the basis for the extensive investigations described in the Blackwell Research Reports on quality illumination.

Porcelain Enamel: More correctly, this type of coating is identified as *vitreous enamel.* It consists of a mineral oxide coating fused to the metal substrate. By the addition of opacifiers, the color and opacity can be varied. The reflectances of white coatings can approach .90. Because the finish is not affected by many acids and nonabrasive cleaners, it is an excellent outdoor type of finish and recommended where extreme environmental conditions are to be experienced.

Position Index: A number assigned to a glare source which is dependent on its position within the field of view. Depending upon the position of the task, any line of sight can be used to determine the position index. The position of the glare source within the visual field can be specified in terms of distances from the eye and along the line of sight. Normally a horizontal line of sight is used for most discomfort glare evaluations.

Preheat Fluorescent Lamp: A fluorescent lamp requiring the use of a starter circuit to preheat the filaments prior to striking the arc. The starting sequence can be performed manually or automatically as with a device known as a starter. The "starting period" lasts for a few seconds after which the arc is struck and light is produced.

Pressure: A type of stress characterized by is uniformity in all directions as distinguished from compressive stress in one direction. Its measure is the force exerted per unit area. For example, the normal atmospheric pressure is 14.7 pounds per square inch. Pressure is usually associated with a decrease in volume, though the opposite effect is sometimes associated with "negative pressure." This latter must be distinguished from the same term sometimes used to denote pressures below atmospheric, that pressure being in such cases taken as an arbitrary zero. *Absolute pressure* is the true pressure of a system to distinguish it from partial or gage pressure and is referred to vacuum as zero. *Gauge pressure* is that pressure indicated by a gauge and shows pressure above the local atmospheric pressure. Manometers measure pressure by using pressure exerted upon a column of liquid—either water or mercury—and are often calibrated to read directly in terms of inches of liquid.

Prism: An optical device of glass or other clear material designed to transmit light by reflection or refraction, depending upon the geometric shape of the prism. The precise direction of propagation of light through a prism is predicated upon flat surfaces and accuracy and sharpness of angles.

Pritchard Telephotometer: A direct reading instrument with a wide range of acceptance angles from 2 degrees down to 6 minutes of an arc, enabling the measurement of direct luminances of 10^{-4} to 10^{-8} footlamberts. Polarized light may be measured because there are no internal reflections of the beam.

Quality of Illumination: The distribution of brightness and color rendition in a visual environment. The term is used in a positive sense and implies that certain attributes (comfort, ease of seeing, safety, and aesthetics for specific visual tasks) are involved.

Quantity of Illumination: For the purposes of illuminating engineering, the quantity of illumination is the time rate of flow of luminous radiation—the total luminous energy which has passed through unit area perpendicular to the beam. It is usually expressed in lumens per unit area or footcandles.

Quantum Theory: A modern form of the corpuscular theory of the nature of light, advanced by Planck and others, that the energy of radiation emitted or absorbed is concentrated in discrete quanta or photons each with an energy in ergs of 6.624×10^{-27} times the frequency of the radiation in cycles per second.

Quartz: The most common variety of silicon dioxide occurring in the natural state as grains or in masses of white or gray color. Pure crystalline quartz is colorless and is called *rock crystal*. Quartz is relatively a hard material, easy to polish and has a wider spectral transmittance than glass, being transparent to ultraviolet and infrared radiation. It finds many uses in optical instruments particularly those which use polarized light. The low thermal expansion at high temperatures makes quartz an ideal material for use in small lamp envelopes, as in the quartz-iodine lamp.

Quartz-Iodine Lamps: A tungsten filament lamp in quartz envelope utilizing the halogen regenerative cycle to provide excellent lamp lumen maintenance together with small bulb size. It is classed as an incandescent lamp. Sometimes referred to as a halogen lamp.

Raceway: According to the NEC, a raceway is intended to mean "any channel for holding wires, cables or busbars, which is designed expressly for and used solely for the purpose." Raceways may be made of metal or insulating material, and the term includes rigid metal conduit, flexible metal conduit, electrical metallic tubing, underfloor raceways, cellular metal floor raceways, surface metal raceways, wireways, and bussways. To meet the U.L. requirements for raceways, factors such as metal thickness, corrosion protection, number, size and type of conductors permitted, and the method of installation would be taken into account to determine acceptability as a raceway.

Radiance: The radiant flux per unit of projected area and unit solid angle either leaving a surface at a given point in a given direction or arriving at a given point from a given direction.

Radiant Energy: Energy traveling in the form of electromagnetic waves.

Radiant Flux: The time rate of flow of radiant energy.

Radio Interference: Electrical discharge lamps generate energy in the radio frequency portion of the electromagnetic spectrum which manifests itself as noise in the operation of radio frequency instruments. This interference may be radiated directly by the lamps, or a portion of this energy may be conducted back into the supply lines directly into instrumentation or reradiated from such wiring. There are three possibilities for controlling such interference: using an optical material or screening across the luminaire opening to attenuate the radio interference, using of an insertion filter into the supply line and thus preventing the feedback of the interference, using both of these methods together. The standard ballast as a component normally does not cause interference, although its design may be partially effective in impeding the feedback of interference. The amount of attenuation of such interference will depend upon the requirements and the choice of components. Commercially available components can offer sufficient attenuation to satisfy most criteria for interference free "suppression."

Radiometer: Instrumental photometers designed to measure the radiant flux commonly from a lamp, over a wide range of frequencies. They may be selective or nonselective. Normally the requirement is to determine the extent of radiation in the visible region of the spectrum, in which case they may be color-corrected to meet the standard spectral luminosity curve.

Rapid Start Lamps: Fluorescent lamps which, in conjunction with appropriate ballasts, eliminate the need for auxiliary starting aids to affect lamp operation. A short preheating period is automatically injected into the lamp starting cycle by ballast design after which period (usually one or two seconds), the lamp arc is struck and normal operation begins. The lamp filaments are designed to be continuously heated through normal operation with very low losses. This rapid-start principle of continuously heated filaments enables the design of flashing and dimming circuits.

Ray: The direction of propagation of electromagnetic waves, as of light.

Reactor: An electrical device, the primary purpose of which is to introduce reactance into an electrical circuit, e.g., capacitor and choke coil. In this respect, a ballast serves as a reactor.

Recessed Lighting: The general meaning is a luminaire mounted into a recess in a ceiling so that its luminous surface is usually flush with the ceiling finishing material. According to the NEC, a recessed fixture is one which is mounted in a similar manner into the structural ceiling of a building.

Recommended Illumination Levels: These are illumination levels for a variety of tasks as recommended by the IES. They are minimum levels on the task and are based upon data evolved from the Blackwell Research Projects and those of the IES Committee on Quantity and Quality of Illumination. For a complete listing of recommended footcandle levels, see Chapter 6.

Reflectance: The ratio of the flux reflected by a surface or medium to the incident flux. The reflectance of a surface can be diffuse, specular, or a combination of both. Gloss is a measure of the degree of specularity as compared to diffuse reflection of a surface.

Reflected Glare: Glare resulting from specular reflections of high brightness in polished or glossy surfaces in the field of view. It is usually associated with reflections within the task or in close proximity to the task.

Reflection Factor: The reflectance of a material expressed as a percentage of the incident light on that material.

Refraction: The process by which the direction of a ray of light is changed as it passes obliquely from one medium into another of different refractive index.

Refraction Index: The phase velocity of light in vacuum, divided by the phase velocity of the same light in a specified medium. The Refraction Index may also be stated as the ratio of the size of the angle of incidence to the size of the angle of refraction. Because the refraction index of air is only 1.00029, the refraction index is frequently measured with respect to air rather than to vacuum.

Room Cavity: The cavity formed by the work plane, the plane of the luminaires, and the wall surfaces between these planes.

Room Cavity Ratio: A number calculated from the same basic formula dependent on room dimensions and proportions of length, width and height.

Scissors Curve: A criterion of limiting luminances of a luminaire, presented in graph form. The curves for limiting luminances represent straight lines on the graph which cross a common point representing 250 footlamberts at 75° viewing angle (nadir $= 0°$).

Scotopic Vision: Vision that takes place through the medium of the rods of the retina only and therefore represents vision at very low levels of brightness.

Selenium Cell: Also Barrier Layer Cell and Photovoltaic Cell. A device used to detect and/or measure radiant energy by generating a potential across the material layers in its construction.

Semidirect: C.I.E. luminaire distribution classification having flux distribution of 10 to 40% above and 10 to 40% below the horizontal.

Sensible Heat: See Heat Sensible.

Shielding Angle: The angle between the horizontal line through the light center and the line of sight usually below this line at which the bare source first becomes visible. This is in direct opposition to the cut-off angle which would be the angular measurement from nadir or the vertical line through the lamp source and the line of sight usually above this line at which the bare source becomes invisible.

Short-Arc Lamps: High-pressure gas discharge lamps having an arc length which is small compared to the size of the electrodes. Due to the concentrated light source and small size of envelope, short-arc lamp bulbs are usually made of clear fused quartz. Lamps are commonly designed for dc operation.

Slimline Lamps: A fluorescent or electrical discharge lamp named after the small diameters of lamp bulb sizes initially introduced. Later manufacture introduced larger standard diameters of 1.5 inches. This lamp requires no preheating of filaments.

Solid Angle: The ratio of an area on the surface of a sphere to the square of radius of the sphere, expressed in steradians.

Spacing to Mounting Height Ratios: A ratio of the distance between luminaire centers to the mounting height above the work plane.

Spectral Energy Distribution, Of a Light Source: Data of energy versus wavelength usually shown as a curve giving the power distribution through the spectrum of the light source with the power as ordinate and the wavelength as abscissa.

Specular Angle: Is that angle of reflectance that is equal to the angle of incidence.

Specular, Reflection: That process by which incident flux is redirected at the specular angle.

Specular, Transmission: That process by which incident flux passes through a material without scattering.

Steradian (unit solid angle): A solid angle subtending an area on the surface of a sphere equal to the square of the radius.

Stroboscope Effect: When rapidly moving objects are observed under fluorescent lighting, blurred "ghost" images may be observed. This effect is caused by cyclic variation in light output, and varies with lamps depending on color, types of phosphors, and ballast circuit. The cyclic variation of light output is known as *flicker* and the *Flicker Index* is an indication of the degree of stroboscopic effect to be expected from a fluorescent lamp.

Subjective Brightness: The subjective attribute of any light sensation giving rise to the precept of luminous intensity, including the whole scale of qualities of bright, light, brilliant, dim, or dark. For photometric quantities, the term *luminance* is preferable, thus reserving *brightness* for the subjective quantity.

Thermal Protection: For a ballast, a means of preventing excessive temperatures within a ballast by the use of a thermally sensitive device usually mounted within a ballast and which, when subjected to temperatures above a preset limit, will interrupt the electrical supply to the ballast. Such devices may be automatically reset or of a "one time" design. They may also be current sensitive.

Toroidal Distribution: A candlepower distribution curve approximating the shape of a toroid or a doughnut. Line sources such as fluorescent lamps have a toroidal distribution.

Transmittance (Transmission Factor): The ratio of the flux transmited by a medium to the flux incident on its surface.

Tristimulus Values, of a Light: The amounts of each of three primary sources required to match the color of the light. This specification is usually stated in C.I.E. trichromatic coordinates of x, y and z factors.

Tungsten, Iodine Lamps: Incandescent lamps employing the tungsten-iodine regenerative cycle to provide extended filament life, excellent lamp maintenance, and, small lamp size by the use of quartz envelopes. Iodine is a member of the halogen family of elements and, for this reason, the lamp is also shown as a halogen or tungsten halogen lamp.

Ultra-Violet Radiant Energy: That portion of the electromagnetic spectrum immediately below the visible blue end of the spectrum and comprising a band 10 to 380 nanometers. This band, for practical purposes, is divided into the following bands:

Ozone-producing	180 to 220 nanometers
Bactericidal	220 to 300 nanometers
Erythemal (skin-tan)	280 to 320 nanometers
"Black Light"	320 to 400 nanometers

Uniformity of Illumination: In predicting the illumination level by the lumen method, it is desirable that the maximum and minimum levels do not vary by more than one-sixth above or below the average illumination level throughout the work area.

Unit Solid Angle: See Steradian.

Utilance (Formerly Utilization Factor): The ratio of the luminous flux received on the work plane to that emitted by the luminaire. Utilance multipled by the luminaire efficiency is the coefficient of utilization.

Veiling Reflection: Specular or regular reflections superimposed upon diffuse reflections from an object which partially or totally obscure the details to be seen by reducing contrast, sometimes called reflected glare.

Visual Acuity: The ability to distinguish fine details.

Visual Field: The focus of objects or points in space which can be perceived when the head and eyes are kept fixed. The field may be monocular or binocular. In human vision, the field, normally binocular, is approximately $60°$ in radius— somewhat larger than it would be for monocular vision.

Visual Performance: The quantitative assessment of the performance of a task, taking into consideration speed and accuracy.

Visual Purple (Rhodopsin): A chemical substance found in the rods of the retina in the eye which upon exposure to light breaks down into "retinine" and "opsin" and finally into "Vitamin A." It is generally accepted that this photochemical/chemical cycle makes it possible for the photoreceptors (rods) to generate nerve impulses when exposed to light. A similar process is believed to take place within the cones.

Visual Surround: All portions of the visual field except the task.

Visual Task: Those details and objects which must be seen for the performance of a given activity, including the immediate background of the details and objects.

Visual Task Evaluator: An apparatus designed to investigate the level of illumination and the degree of contrast necessary to achieve a specified level of visual performance. The Visual Task Evaluator provides a useful method for relative actual visual tasks to a standard laboratory target and has been the basis for determining the recommended footcandle levels for a large variety of tasks as investigated by Blackwell.

Wavelength, Complementary: In illumination, the wavelength of radiant energy of a single frequency that, when combined in suitable proportion with the light, matches the color of the reference standard.

Wavelength, Dominant: In illumination, the wavelength of radiant energy of a single frequency that, when combined in suitable proportion with the radiant energy of the reference standard, matches the color of the light.

Wavelength, Units of Illumination:

Angstrom—equal to 10^{-10} meter
Nanometer—equal to 10^{-9} meter, formally called millicicron
Micron—equal to 10^{-6} meter

Weighted Ordinate Method: An alternate method for determining the C.I.E. specification for a color in terms of C.I.E. coordinates, x, y and Y.

Work Plane: The plane, usually horizontal, at which work is to be done and at which illumination is to be specified and measured.

Xenon Lamp: An electrical discharge lamp, usually of small arc length, utilizing xenon as the lamp fill gas. The use of xenon fill gas enables the design of a lamp with a relatively short warm-up time before full operating pressure and light output are achieved.

Yellowing Factor: A rating applied specifically to the discoloration of plastic materials due to exposure to radiation such as from a fluorescent lamp. This method of predicting the "in service" performance of plastic materials in lighting materials is based upon the test method outlined by the American Society for Testing and Materials, #D1925-62T, entitled *Yellowness Index of Transparent and Opaque Plastics*. Present test methods used to determine the Yellowness Index or Yellowing Factor have modified certain elements of the test method, as well as the method for evaluation in an attempt to simulate conditions, more closely in regard to exposure to fluorescent lamps.

Zonal-Cavity Method of Illumination Calculations: A method of calculating the average footcandle level in a room. This method based upon the cavity concept, in which the room is divided into three cavities: the ceiling cavity, the floor cavity, and the room cavity. This modern treatment of room proportions results in a new system of room cavity ratio evaluations which permit more accurate application of interflectance data and the solution of problems involving the interference of partitions, beams, and other forms of obstructions in otherwise empty rooms.

Zonal Interflectance Method of Calculating the Coefficient of Utilization: A method of calculation based upon the zonal distribution of lumens from a fixture. Coefficients of Utilization calculated and identified by this method are not suitable for use with the Zonal-Cavity Method of Illumination Calculation, which requires that the Coefficients of Utilization be calculated in conformance with the Room Cavity concept and are identified as by the Zonal-Cavity Interflectance Method.

Zonal Lumens: The flux distribution from a fixture is divided into $10°$ radial zones. The zonal lumens are the amount of lumens falling on the surface of a hypothetical sphere divided into $10°$ belts or zones.

Index